The Search for Common Ground

The Search for Common Ground

AN INQUIRY INTO THE BASIS OF
MAN'S EXPERIENCE OF COMMUNITY

Howard Thurman

Friends United Press

Richmond, Indiana

Library of Congress Cataloging-in-Publication Data

Thurman, Howard, 1900-1981.
    The search for common ground.

       1.   Identification (Religion)   I.   Title
BV4509.5.T49 1986   128   86-25807
ISBN 0-913408-94-8

To our grandchildren
Emily . . . Anton . . . Suzanne:
One single experience—
Seeking and finding the common ground

Contents

Foreword

My own well-thumbed copy of this book contains the following inscription: "the threads of life weave their way mysteriously." Indeed they do. The threads which trail out from Howard Thurman and his book weave a rich tapestry in which my own life and those of people I care about are intricately emeshed.

The inscription is from Colin and Joan Diver, two Bostonians who began as central figures in my own book–*Common Ground: A Turbulent Decade in the Lives of Three American Families*–and became close and valued friends. At one level, the note in Joan's careful, cursive hand, might refer only to the striking similarities–in title and theme–between Dr. Thurman's book and my own.

But the threads to which the Divers refer are more intricate than that. Joan's father, Dr. George Makechnie, met Howard Thurman in the early 1950s while both men were on the faculty at Boston University, Thurman as Dean of Marsh Chapel, Makechnie as Dean of the Sargent College of Physical Education and Physical Therapy. Born a Baptist, George Makechnie had long rankled at the rigid dogma of his faith; when he heard Thurman preach at Marsh Chapel he was delighted by the way his supple homilies transcended traditional bounds, "neither male nor female, Black

nor White, Protestant nor Catholic." Soon the black theologian
and the white educator discovered that they were kindred spirits.
The two couples began exchanging visits. Finding that each had
been married on the same day–June 12–they held an annual
anniversary dinner. Before long, their families developed a
profound rapport.

For Joan Makechnie, Thurman was "Uncle Howard," a strong
but gentle presence in her parents' home, a towering figure in the
pulpit on Sundays, a spiritual guide and mentor who made her see
the unity of all human experience. So when Joan, fresh out of
Wheaton College in 1965, married Colin Diver, a recent graduate
of Amherst, they asked Howard Thurman to preside. To
underline the symbolic importance of that decision, they said
they wanted him to perform the ceremony in Marsh Chapel on
June 12. Yes, the threads of life weave their way mysteriously.

I was snared by those threads a decade later when, embarking
on my book about the intersecting lives of three Boston families, I
asked the Divers to introduce me to people who had helped to
shape their worldview. High on their list was Howard Thurman,
who by then had left Boston University to return to San Francisco.

One day in December 1976, I paid a call on the aged theologian
in his dark, book-lined study overlooking the shimmering bay. It
was there that he told me the astonishing story of his life: born the
grandchild of a slave, reared in racially segregated Daytona
Beach, Florida, where he raked the lawns of the wealthy whites,
and where one day a white child jabbed him with a pin, and said,
"That didn't hurt you; you can't feel."

But he did feel–and feel intensely. Leaning against a giant oak in
his backyard or strolling along the beach to find companionship
with the ocean, the sun, the moon and the stars, he sensed very
early on the "sacredness and interrelationship of all life."

Through the years, he deepened that intuitive sense of
universality into a philosophical conviction that "life is against all
dualism, life is one...Always, against all that fragments and
shatters, and against all things that separate and divide within and
without, life labors to meld together into a single harmony."

A visit to Mahatma Gandhi in 1935 convinced him of the
powerful energy which could be released by non-violence.
Through the years as a professor at Howard University; as founder

and pastor of San Francisco's interfaith, interracial Church for the Fellowship of All Peoples; and then at Boston University from 1953 to 1965, he wove these strands into a doctrine he called "the love ethic," in which he cried out, "I want to be more loving in my heart...Keep open the door of thy heart; it matters not how many doors are closed against thee." Nothing he wrote, however, is more telling than this slim volume, conceived in the aftermath of Martin Luther King's assassination, when whites and blacks, rich and poor, southerners and northerners, seemed ready to abandon their search for a unitary society and to huddle in little ghettos of the spirit, proclaiming their irreconcilability.

Howard Thurman understood the need of all living beings to proclaim the uniqueness of their own experience, to build protective walls around their community until they can feel secure in their identity. But, he warned, "that community cannot feed for long on itself; it can only flourish where always the boundaries are giving way to the coming of others from beyond them." We belong to each other, he said, and we if shut ourselves away we diminish ourselves.

Howard Thurman died in 1981 at the age of 81, but his spirit survives–in these pages and in the hearts of all who brushed against him. It lives, I know, in George Makechnie, in Joan and Colin Diver, and in me. The threads of life, indeed, weave their way mysteriously.

J. Anthony Lukas
New York, N.Y. 1986

Preface

This particular book has been more than four years in the making. The journey has led me into areas of exploration somewhat foreign to my immediate academic interests. It was a wary experience getting the feel of an unfamiliar vocabulary as the concept unfolded before me. When I finished the first five chapters, my mind came to a dead end. For a long time it was not clear to me what the meaning of my pursuit for community would be in terms of the present tensions between black and white in American society.

From my childhood I have been on the scent of the tie that binds life at a level so deep that the final privacy of the individual would be reinforced rather than threatened. I have always wanted to be *me* without making it difficult for you to be *you*. When I completed this manuscript, I was struck by the feeling that here I had set down the case in rather formal terms, for what reveals itself is my lifelong working paper. What is suggested and often stated in previous books, such as *The Creative Encounter, Jesus and the Disinherited,* and *Footprints of a Dream,* in the present volume comes full circle in a wider context, rooted in the life process itself.

The paradox of conscious life is the ultimate issue here. On the one hand is the absolute necessity for the declaration that states unequivocally the uniqueness of the private life, the awful sense of being an isolate, independent and alone, the great urgency to savor one's personal flavor—to stand over against all the rest of life in contained affirmation. While on the other hand is the necessity to feel oneself as a primary part of all of life, sharing at every level of awareness a dependence upon the same elements in nature, caught up in the ceaseless rhythm of living and dying, with no final immunity against a common fate that finds and holds all living things.

In a sense, therefore, I have been writing this book all my life. Over and over again I have asked myself: What is the common ground that floats the private adventure of the individual or solitary life? Is it merely conceptual, is it only the great idea, the hunger of the heart rationalized into a transcendent God-idea, concept, or notion? Or are these but the scent of the eternal in all living things, perhaps reaching its apotheosis in man, and in the religious man in particular?

Such questions become a personal crisis for a black man living in American society in the last decades of the twentieth century. At this moment there is a vast urgency for separateness, for isolating the black experience from the American experience in general, and establishing on that basis a grand windbreak behind which the black community can define and articulate its unique identity as a self-conscious participant in American and, indeed, world society. All of this is interpreted as a necessary technique of survival by which both the private and the public character can be defined. In the intensity of the urgency, the lines of separation between black and white are seen psychologically as being absolute, and everything in the past that is contrariwise must be regarded as false, degrading, and evil.

This book is one man's statement of how he deals with the ambiguities created by the existential period in which his life must be lived. There is a relentless ambivalence for me in honoring the sources of my own integrity and inspiration while at the same time recognizing their relevance to the times in which I am now living. In the first chapter, I define the meaning of the search for the common ground in a broad and fundamentally philosophical context, in language that a thoughtful reader will not find too involved or abstruse. I urge the reader to follow the thread of the basic thesis as set forth there.

The second chapter examines the "racial memory" as set forth in the query accounts of creation that tell of a "time when" there was harmony and community among all living things as a part of the givenness of the Creator to his creation. It was a time of the "wholeness of innocence" with no active, divisive principle at work. That innocence was lost, and the long struggle for community familiar to mankind was begun. This racial memory is universal and is not unique to any particular cultural, religious, or ethnic origin.

The third chapter deals with the character of the search as found implicit in all living structures, including man and some of the problems created by his autonomy and self-consciousness.

The fourth chapter interprets the meaning of the search as defined in Utopias. In the dreams of the seers and prophets, harmony, by definition, is built into the structured societies. What we see is a deliberate creation of the dreamer and an echo of what he seeks in the immediate world in which his life is being lived out.

The fifth chapter is a look at the common consciousness binding all living things and the way in which the separate forms, dividing one kind of life or one particular expression of life from another, seem to be final and absolute. Attention is given to the experience of going behind the division, for instance, between man and animals to discover their common ground as a true basis of communication and understanding between them.

The final chapter explores the meaning of the search for identity, which is the mood and necessity for the black man, who, for the first time in American society, is beginning to think of himself as an integral part of the society in his own right. This intensive and increasing polarization in the society has brought the issue of identity into sharp focus for minorities, thereby allowing them to reject all arbitrary social classifications arising from the larger society.

For the religious man, there rides always on his horizon a timeless, transcendent monitor by which not only is the direction of his life somehow guided but also by which he is stabilized in the midst of the contradictions of his experience. But this does not release him from the necessity of seeking always to locate his profoundest religious insights in the very structure of his life as a living human being, spawned from the womb of the earth, and as a participant in that which sustains and supports all life on the planet. Ultimately, all the dualisms of his experience as a creature must exhaust themselves in a corroborating unity fundamental to life and not merely dependent upon that which transcends life by whatever name he seeks to patronize it.

I dreamed I saw a land. And on the hills walked brave women and brave men, hand in hand. And they looked into each other's eyes, and they were not afraid.

And I saw the women also hold each other's hands.
And I said to him beside me, "What place is this?"
And he said, "This is heaven."
And I said, "Where is it?"
And he answered, "On earth."
And I said, "When shall these things be?"
And he answered, "In the Future."

—Olive Schreiner

Acknowledgments

I express my appreciation to the many creative minds that have thought deeply and written clearly in the various areas which I have explored. A bibliography of direct sources appears at the end of the book.

Joyful appreciation goes to the following: my secretary, Alice Ratner, who, in addition to the typing and retyping of the entire manuscript, gave of her time in checking references and making significant suggestions about documentation, etc.; Mary May Tekse who typed the final chapter from the handwritten copy and who used her skill in checking the manuscript for errors that played hide and seek in the pages of the material; Mrs. Anne Chiarenza, my daughter, who read the entire manuscript with the skill of a copyeditor and the sensitivity of the younger generation; and finally, my wife, Sue Bailey Thurman, who insisted that this was an important and timely statement to be made and that I *must* make it.

The Search for Common Ground

Concerning the Search

An old man with a double-bit axe
Is caretaker at the Gore place. The cattle, except a
    few wild horns, died in that fire; the horses
Graze high up the dark hill; nobody ever comes to the
    infamous house; the pain, the hate and the love
Have left no ghost. Old men and gray hawks need solitude,
Here it is deep and wide.

    "Winter and summer," the old man says, "rain and the
    drought;
Peace creeps out of war, war out of peace; the stars
    rise and they set; the clouds go north
And again they go south. —Why does God hunt in circles?
    Has he lost something? Is it possible—himself?
In the darkness between the stars did he lose himself
    and become godless, and seeks—himself?"

"Does God exist? —No doubt of that," the old man says.
    "The cells of my old camel of a body,

Because they feel each other and are fitted together—
    through nerves and blood feel each other—all the
    little animals
Are the one man: there is not an atom in all the universes

"But feels every other atom; gravitation, electromagnetism,
    light, heat, and the other
Flamings, the nerves in the night's black flesh, flow
    them together; the stars, the winds and the people:
    one energy,
One existence, one music, one organism, one life, one
    God: star-fire and rock-strength, the sea's cold
    flow
And man's dark soul."

"Not a tribal nor an anthropoid God.
Not a ridiculous projection of human fears, needs,
    dreams, justice and Love-lust."

"A conscious God? —The question has no importance.
    But I am conscious: where else
Did this consciousness come from? Nobody that I know
    of ever poured grain from an empty sack.
And who, I would say, but God, and a conscious one,
Ended the chief war-makers with their war, so humorously,
    such accurate timing, and such
Appropriate ends? . . ."

—ROBINSON JEFFERS*

There is something so private and personal about an act of
thought that the individual may very easily seem to be a private
island on a boundless human sea. To experience one's self is to enter
into a solitary world that is one's unique possession and that can
never be completely and utterly shared. Here is the paradox. A
man is always threatened in his very ground by a sense of isolation,
by feeling himself cut off from his fellows. Yet he can never sepa-

---

* Reprinted by permission of Jeffers Literary Properties.

rate himself from his fellows, for mutual interdependence is characteristic of all of life.

The need to care for and the need to be cared for is another expression of the same basic idea. It is unnecessary to resort to moral or religious authority for a mandate or for an injunction. Such needs are organic, whatever may be their psychological or spiritual derivatives. Therefore, whenever the individual is cut off from the private and personal nourishment from other individuals or from particular individuals, the result is a wasting away, a starvation, a failure of his life to be sustained and nourished. Studies show that some fifty years ago, when an effort was made to track down the cause of the death of more than half of the children who died during the first year of life, it was found to be due to a disease known as *marasmus*. This disease was also known as infantile atrophy or devility, coming from the Greek word *marasmós*, meaning "wasting away." The discovery was made that such babies were not neglected as far as their physical care, cleanliness, and the like were concerned. Rather, what was lacking was the free and easy access of the child to the psychic nourishment made possible through mother love. Perhaps it is largely for this reason that hospitals today keep the infant for as short a period as possible. When the real mother is not available, mother-love substitutes are provided. I have heard of an instance in which a mother's heartbeat was put on a tape and the sound amplified through the public address system in a hospital nursery for the benefit of all the babies.

The human spirit cannot abide the enforced loneliness of isolation. We literally feed on each other; where this nourishment is not available, the human spirit and the human body—both—sicken and die. It is not an overstatement that the purpose of all of the arrangements and conventions that make up the formal and informal agreements under which men live in society is to nourish one another *with* one another. The safeguards by which individuals or groups of men establish the boundaries of intimate and collective belonging are meant ultimately to guarantee self-nourishment. All of these are but social expressions of the underlying experience of life with itself. Life feeds on life; life is nourished by life. It is life's experience with itself that establishes the ground for the dogma that life is eternal.

To seek nourishment is a built-in urge, an ingredient of life in its simplest or most complex manifestations. The creative push that expresses itself in this way is the manner by which life realizes itself. The descriptive term that characterizes such behavior is "actualizing potential." Wherever life is observed this is its primary activity or business. In this sense all life is engaged in goal-seeking.

The degree to which the potential in any expression of life is actualized marks the extent tc which such an expression of life experiences wholeness, integration, community. The clue to community can be found in the inner creative activity of living substances. The more highly developed the organism, the more pronounced seems to be the manifestation of the clue. Cells and organisms always show certain characteristics of direction, persistence, and adaptability in their efforts to realize themselves, to round themselves out, to fulfill themselves, to become, to ripen in integration—in fine, to experience community. The more highly developed the organism, the more plainly manifest are these characteristics.

It seems reasonable to say, then, that the "intent" of creation is that life lives by constantly seeking to realize itself in established forms, patterns, and units. Expressed in this way, it must not be thought that life is static, something that is set, fixed, determined. The key word to remember always is *potential:* that which has not yet come to pass but which is always coming to pass. It is only the potential, the undisclosed, the unfinished that has a future. I find it difficult to think of life apart from the notion of potential; indeed, they seem synonymous. To be sure, life is not finished yet; creation is still going on, not only in the spinning of new worlds, systems, nebulae, and galaxies in the infinitude of space, not only in the invisible world where chemical elements are born and nourished to support conglomerates of matter yet to appear at some far-off moment in time, but also in the human body, which is still evolving, in the human mind, which so slowly loosens its corporal bonds, and in the human spirit, which forever drives to know the truth of itself and of its fellows.

In human society, the experience of community, or realized potential, is rooted in life itself because the intuitive human urge for community reflects a characteristic of all life. In the total panorama of the external world of nature, there seems to be a pattern of structural dependability and continuity, or what may be called an inner logic, that manifests itself in forms, organizational schemes, and in a wide variety of time-space arrangements. The most striking pattern of all is that there seems to be affinity between the human mind and all external forms, a fact that makes an understanding of the world possible for the mind.

The religious basis for such an interpretation of community is the affirmation, which to me is categorical, that the Mind of God realizes Itself in *time,* and that there are observable patterns or sequences in all creation. Thus God is thought of as Creator. From this point of view, all time-space manifestations of substance—in short, all things, even existence itself—are regarded as the Mind of God coming to *Itself* in time and space. This is evident in history and in nature. Existence itself is construed as divine activity. There seems to be a principle of rationality in all existence, and the significance of this can be found in the order in life. True, what seems to be a principle of rationality as expressed in observable order in life may be a limitation of mind itself. Yet it is this assumption of inherent logic in the functioning of the mind that makes comprehension of the external world possible.

I recognize the fact that in using the formal name Creator, I am using anthropomorphic terminology. I do this quite deliberately, because I find it quite impossible to think of action—and this is implicit in the term—as an abstraction. While it is true that when the mind is concerned with something as vast as existence itself, any kind of limitation is paradoxical, if not contradictory; nevertheless, the mind as a thinking entity can only make sense of this complexity by using symbols that can stand for ideas and fields of comprehension. Behind the "thisness and thatness" of experience and observation one has to sense something more. Whatever term is used to express this dimension (also a limiting word) simply extends the boundary; it does not get rid of it. One may use the term *ground* or *infinitude*, or, to borrow a phrase from Northrup, "the undifferentiated aesthetic continuum"; or Eckhart's *nameless nothing* or *Godhead* as he distinguishes it from God; or a contemporary theologian's term, "God above God." All these phrases are an attempt to escape the dilemma of pure existence that, to the mind, is meaningless.

The man who seeks community within his own spirit, who searches for it in his experiences with the literal facts of the external world, who makes this his formal intent as he seeks to bring order out of the chaos of his collective life, is not going against life but will be sustained and supported by life. And for the world of modern man this is crucial. In the conflicts between man and man, between group and group, between nation and nation, the loneliness of the seeker for community is sometimes unendurable. The radical tension between good and evil, as man sees it and feels it, does not have the last word about the meaning of life and the nature of existence. There is a spirit in man and in the world working always against the thing that destroys and lays waste. Always he must know that the contradictions of life are not final or ultimate; he must distinguish between failure and a many-sided awareness so that he will not mistake conformity for harmony, uniformity for synthesis. He will know that for all men to be alike is the death of life in man, and yet perceive the harmony that transcends all diversities and in which diversity finds its richness and significance.

The order in creation and the orderly disorder that seem to characterize what is regarded as random activity in certain aspects of the world external to man, the concepts in the mind that are derivatives of man's experience with his senses, and those other concepts that seem to take their form from the boundless ebb and flow of the imageless tides that wash the shores of the human mind and spirit—all these express an authentic creativity that is Mind at work, and man is an essential part of the order. What is observed as a structure of orderliness or dependability in any and all expressions of life, from the simplest forms to the most complex, is seen most dramatically in the ability of man to create, to conceptualize, to plan, to function purposefully, and to implement in time and space what is idea or thought to the mind. From within the narrow circle of man's mind there can be no thought or action that is not involved in some form of intent—intent as a form of volition, focused or unfocused, deliberate or unconscious. In man's experience with life, within him at all levels and about him in varied manifestations in time-space intervals, he is a part of the world of facts and meaning, suggesting creative intent. It seems reasonable, then, to assume that wherever life is found, evidence of creative intent must also exist in that which is being experienced, reacted to, observed, or studied. One such sign, and the most crucial one, is the way life seeks always to realize itself in wholeness, harmony, and integration within the potential that characterizes the particular expression of life. The most natural question that comes to mind, therefore, whenever men reflect upon or try to rationalize their experiences of life is: How did life get started? What was the beginning of it all?

II

The Search into Beginnings

It is natural that man should concern himself with beginnings. This is a part of the curiosity of the mind. Without it there would be no exploration of the world and there would be no growth. The twin queries that haunt the mind are Why and How—perhaps the order is most often reversed, How and then Why. This is an inherent characteristic of mind; it is not unique to any particular age of man, culture, or society. Contemplation concerning origins is a part of the curiosity of the race.

Such contemplation may arise out of the need to have experience make sense, to make it fit into some kind of order in the simplest and most elementary manner. Or it may express itself out of a kind of sophistication as man seeks to relate to his world meaningfully in an effort to manipulate it to private ends, to control it, or master it in establishing his own emotional security. But whatever may be the reason, the essential characteristic behavior persists as we want to know how the world began, where we came from, and what the meaning of life, and Life, is.

When we examine the various accounts of how the world began,

8

the origin of life in general, and man's work in particular, we are face to face with what has been aptly called the "memory of a lost harmony." One notices immediately that ideas about the origin of man are completely separated from whatever is thought of as the origin of life. The origin of life is never separated from the origin of the world. This is a most intriguing realization. It is as if the sense of common origin is inescapable. Brooding over the bill of particulars of creation there is the notion of an active continuum, or spirit, or vital complex that is being demonstrated. Always the manifestation is an expression of an internal order. What emerges out of the brooding formlessness called chaos, is order. Any part of nature— say, a rock, a tree, or a man—is an expression of order. The relation between a rock, a tree, and a man is also an expression of order. Where the mind cannot see order, it sees chaos. Chaos is always giving way to order as knowledge and insight develop.

The total impact of this concept was brought home to me many years ago. When I was a small boy growing up in Daytona Beach, Florida, I earned money doing various chores. One of my regular chores was to collect discarded newspapers and magazines from certain homes and take them for disposal to the city dump. Once each month there was included one magazine called *The Atlantic Monthly*. It was printed on heavy, enameled paper that made it very hard to burn. But this is not the thing that stands out in my memory most dramatically. No. What remains in my mind most clearly is a full-page advertisement of a Hamilton watch. In the center of the page was a reproduction of Rodin's "Thinker." This picture affected me profoundly. In fact, I was so enamored of it that I tried to reproduce the pose, the stance, the furrowed brow, the chin resting on the flat side of the fist—these became for me hallmarks of thought and profundity. I practiced the pose whenever I had a spare moment and something to lean against. One day, I recall, my mother told my sister to call me to do an errand. I was leaning against the fence perfecting my stance. I told her to tell my mother that I was thinking. Needless to say, I did not repeat that again.

Years later I visited the Metropolitan Museum of Art in New

York City. In the Rodin gallery I saw a reproduction of the "Thinker." As I walked away from the figure, my hands behind me, my head bowed, my mind buried in thought, I suddenly found my way blocked by the base of a pedestal. When I looked up, I was standing in the presence of the back view of Rodin's "Hand of God." Here was the back of the great hand, the long, graceful fingers, three in full view supported by the giant thumb. Slowly I made my way around to the front of the hand and what I saw there transfixed me in my place: the giant hand, and always the mighty thumb, yet deep in the palm of the hand the chaotic stuff of life. In fact, the hand itself seemed to emerge out of a kind of chaotic conglomerate. And yet, from within the hand, coming up out of this stuff of life, were the shapely bodies of human beings. It was as if a dream of order, implicit in chaos itself and yet brooding over *chaos,* were being held in terrible tension over the stuff of life, until the stuff of life began to respond in shape and form, which was but a manifestation of its own potential. Such was the concept of the artist as it realized itself in his medium. In his creation he says to mankind: This is how we came to be. This is my interpretation of the racial memory of a lost harmony.

In the search for truth on the part of astronomers, physicists, geologists, biologists, and other scientists, a wide variety of hypotheses and theories have developed and will continue to develop in all the years that life remains intact on our planet. As Loren C. Eiseley reminds us in an article in *Harper's Magazine* of October 1953, "after having chided the theologist for his reliance on myth and miracle, science found itself in the unenviable position of having to create a mythology of its own: namely, the assumption that what, after long effort, could not be proved to take place today had, in truth, taken place in the primeval past."

In Maria Leach's *The Beginning: Creation Myths Around the World,* the first chapter neatly summarizes the ways in which the scientific mind has dealt with the question of beginnings. The opening paragraph reads: "The *Old Farmer's Almanac* says that the world began at nine o'clock in the morning on Wednesday,

October 26, in the year 4004 B.C. This is the famous date worked out by James Ussher, Arch-bishop of Armagh in Ireland, from his studies of Hebrew chronology."

It is understandable that man would regard his earth as the center of all creation. Given this fact, it is but a step in logic to arrive at a position of human supremacy over all creation. Out of this position, man may conclude that his place in space is the center of all existence or existences. Even the thought that there might be other inhabitants in the worlds and systems beyond our own must have been extremely threatening to the egos of those who first considered such a possibility.

A simple listing of some of the important scientific theories or accounts of the beginning of the world, as outlined in Maria Leach's first chapter, reads as follows: "(1) the nebular hypothesis; (2) the eruption or planetesimal theory; (3) the tidal theory; (4) the collision theory; (5) the catastrophic theory or the story of the big blow-up; (6) the tale of the lonely atoms or the continuous creation theory."

Each of these is an attempt to answer How. Through this process the mind seeks to push back the veil of mystery that shrouds the concept of origin. The mind lives under the duress of a strange and wonderful urgency in this regard. The important thing about such activity is that even though the boundaries or beginnings of existence cannot be definitely established, science has succeeded in pushing them back beyond what at one time were accented limits. And this has added enormously to the scope of the meaning of man's life and the world in which that life finds a crucial part of its meaning.

Here a comment from J. H. Rush's stimulating and creative book *The Dawn of Life* seems relevant: "What this groping into the past has given us is nothing less than a radically new way of thinking about the universe and our place in it. To my mind, this new approach is the most fundamental of all the changes that science has brought to our lives and thoughts, the most far-reaching in its implications for our understanding of nature and ourselves. It is the principle of evolution."

Since then, according to Dr. Rush, Life finds it reassuring for its purposes not to think of a beginning—or better, *the* beginning—but rather to think of Beginning—a vast series of creative pushes, each one after the manner of its own "idiom" or genius, as it were. Of course, such theorizing does not preclude the notion of a boundless extension of a vibrant continuum from which moves an unnumbered series of Beginnings, always with the possibility that a Beginning may beget a Beginning *ad infinitum*.

What is relevant here is that there is implicit in all these probable developments an inherent order, harmony, integration. This is not as formal acts of consciousness but rather as the pattern or characteristic of the way the creations are formed. It is not necessary to say that it is *the* way the creations are fashioned.

The scientific theories leave out any elements that would indicate a notion of intrinsic purpose or design. They seem to want to deal with the matter of beginnings without introducing the idea of a Creator or the utterly religious term, God. Any such notions are expressed, if at all, by implication. This is as it should be. For science is but one of the moods of the human spirit. "It does not imply that the other moods are fatuous or futile; it does not hold that the truths it enables men to discover are the only truths."

In the creation accounts that have grown or developed out of the seedbed of culture and the spiritual and religious aspiration of the race, something is in evidence that is outside the range and perspective of science. An attempt is made to account for more than the external world of nature, or the elements that make up the natural environment of man. Nothing less than facing the issue of Why is worthy of being transmitted from generation to generation in myriad forms among all the children of men wherever they are found. Here we come upon the creation myths; here we get fleeting and sometimes sustained views of the Creator at work, fashioning the world and bringing into consciousness a thing called life and the living experience.

It is in many of these accounts that the concept of *intent* appears.

In practically every recorded instance the Creator—or, in some instances, the Creators—has something in mind that he seeks to bring to pass in the act of creation. This does not become apparent until, in the sequence of creation, *man* appears. At that moment the organic harmony in the interrelatedness of all creation becomes a part of the *quality* of life itself, a part of the experienced intent of all living things. And it reaches its most impressive articulation in the behavior of human beings. When life appears, it is already committed to realizing itself by the kind of inner harmony and integration that is the way life reproduces itself and persists. "The fullness of time" is a suggestive phrase, meaning the experience of community within an organism when its issue comes forth and makes a bid for the continuity of the form.

I shall now examine two remarkable creation accounts, the first as found in the Judeo-Christian religious tradition, the second as expressed in the creation myth of the Hopi Indians. Let me caution the reader that I have no desire to do violence to any man's particular religious faith. I am simply putting the story of Adam and Eve in the Garden of Eden, as found in the Book of Genesis, in the perspective of the creation account as it has occurred throughout human history. In this sense, the Genesis story is a creation myth —one of many. In explaining my use of the term "myth," I cannot do better than give the definition as found in Webster's *New Intercollegiate Dictionary,* which is sufficiently simple so as to avoid any detailed excursion into anthropology: "A myth is a story, the origin of which is forgotten, ostensibly historical but usually such as to explain some practice, belief, institution or natural phenomenon." The myth, therefore, undertakes to answer a real question about currently experienced, continuous events in the common life. In the creation myth, which is a part of our religious heritage, the question that it tries to answer is universal: How did the world get started; how did it come into being in the first instance? How was man born originally when there were no parents? How did man and all his difficulties start to evolve?

The author or the authors of Genesis tell the following story: On the sixth day of creation, after God created light and made time and space, matter in all its forms, organic and inorganic,

God said, "Let the earth bring forth the living creatures after his kind, cattle and creeping things and beasts of the earth after his kind." And it was so . . . And God saw that it was good. Then God said, "Let us make man in our image after our likeness and let him have dominion over the fish of the sea, and over the fowl of the air, and over the cattle, and over all the earth, and over every creeping thing that creepeth upon the earth." So God created man in his own image . . . male and female created He them.

And the Lord God took the man, and put him into the Garden of Eden to dress it and to keep it. And the Lord God commanded the man, saying, "Of every tree of the garden thou mayst freely eat; but of the tree of the knowledge of good and evil, thou shalt not eat of it: for in the day that thou eatest thereof thou shalt surely die.

The account continues with the idyllic picture of harmony, of community, of tranquility. So influential has the symbolism of the Garden of Eden become in our heritage that when we wish to describe something utterly beautiful and truthful, we say that it is like the Garden of Eden. And by this we mean quite concretely that here is community, wholeness, harmony, with no invasion of the divisiveness out of which discord, disharmony, dissent arise. But it is the harmony of innocence, a harmony that is given as a part of the givenness of the Creator to His creation.

But the author is not through. He says:

The serpent said unto the woman, "Hath God said,
'Ye shall not eat of every tree of the Garden.'"
And the woman said unto the serpent,
"We may eat of the fruit of the trees of the Garden, But of the fruit of the tree which is in the midst of the Garden, God has said,
'Ye shall not eat of it, neither shall ye taste it, lest ye die.'"

And the serpent said—to paraphrase—How stupid can you be? don't you know why God told you this? He knows that if you eat the fruit of the tree you will become just as He is. And then you will be autonomous. He will not be able to control you.

So the woman was convinced and tried to convince Adam and thus make her action binding for him as well. Adam ate the fruit of the tree of knowledge of good and evil, shattering the community of innocence. Strife, discord, enmity, disharmony, suffering, violence—all of these flowed, and they were construed as being at variance with the intent of the Creator in the creation or making of life.

In this creation account Adam is innocent, but he has the potential of behavior that will destroy his innocence. He also has the potential of harmony, and this is a part of the dialectical dimension of his nature. This former potential is epitomized in Eve, who is a part of Adam. Thus Adam has the potential for harmony and its maintenance as well as the potential for the disruption of harmony. When the potential for disharmony is actualized in Adam by his volitional act contrary to the Creator's intent, he loses his *sense of community* with the rest of creation. He loses his innocence, and in the loss of his innocence, for the first time, he becomes a responsible creature—responsible to the Creator, for it is the Creator's intent, in creating him, that he has violated; now he is also responsible to himself for his actions.

Or it may be said that in Adam innocence is given; the state of innocence that is given makes it clear that Adam is as if he were fresh born, as according to the account he is. This potential is actualized without achievement or struggle. He experiences a view of what his life ought to be and in fact is; but, when he violates the intent of the Creator inherent in him, he separates himself from that experience. He is forced now to win it, to achieve it by his own struggle. As long as the potential is a fact given in his creation, Adam is an active participant in community along with all creation. There is no responsibility for action so long as he functions out of innocence.

In the creation myth of the Hopi Indians* the name given to the First World created by the Creator Taiowa was Tokpela, or Endless

*From *Book of the Hopi* by Frank Waters. Copyright © 1963 by Frank Waters. All Rights Reserved. Quotations reprinted by permission of The Viking Press, Inc.

Space. Before the existence of this First World there was only the Creator. "All else was endless space. There was no beginning, and no end, no time, no shape, no life." Time and form and shape—all substance existed only in the mind of the Creator.

His first act was to conceive the finite, the bounded, the limited. All "thisness" and "thatness" came into being by his projection. Hence the finite was first a concept. In order to make the finite manifest itself or establish an existence in its own authenticity or right, he created as his first act Sotuknang, saying to him: "I have created you, the first power and instrument as a person, to carry out my plan for life in endless space. I am your Uncle: you are my Nephew. Go now and lay out these universes in proper order so they may work *harmoniously* with one another according to my plan."

Sotuknang went to work to accomplish what the Creator intended. He brought solid substance out of endless space and gave to it shape and form and established it as nine universal kingdoms divided as follows: one each for the Creator and himself and seven others for the life that was yet to come.

Taiowa was pleased. Then he ordered Sotuknang to accomplish the same ends with waters, which he placed on the surfaces of the universes in an equal manner. The waters were divided equally among the universes—half solid and half water.

Next, the nephew was directed to create forces of air to surround the waters with peaceful movement. Each universe had great forces of air arranged into *gentle order* and *rhythm* around each universe.

Taiowa was pleased. He then ordered his nephew to create life and its movement to round out the four parts of a universal plan.

After this Sotuknang went to Tokpela, the First World, and there he created woman to be his helper. He named her Kokyangwuti, Spider Woman. As soon as she came to life she queried, "Why am I here?"—always the persistent question of the human spirit. The nephew said, "Look about you. Here is this earth we have created. It has shape and substance, direction and time, a beginning and an end. But there is no life upon it. We see no joyful movement. We hear no joyful sounds. What is life without sound or movement? So you have been given the power to help us create this life. You have been given the knowledge, wisdom, and love to bless all the beings you create. That is why you are here." She had been created to create.

The Spider Woman obeyed. She mixed earth with her saliva and molded it into two twin beings. She proceeded to cover them with a white cape of creative wisdom and sang the Creation Song over them. As soon as she uncovered them, the twins sat up and asked the same question: "Who are we? Why are we here?"

Then the Spider Woman said to the one on the right: "You are Poqanghoya and you are to help keep this world in *order* when life is put upon it. Go now around all the world and put your hands upon the earth so that it will become fully solidified. This is your duty." Order had to be grounded as integral in the earth.

To the twin on the left she said, "You are Palongawhoya and you are to help keep this world in order when life is put upon it. This is your duty now; go about all the world and send out sound so that it may be heard throughout the land. When this is heard you will be known as Echo, for all sound echoes the Creator."

The twins obeyed. Mountains and valleys were fashioned as the earth was firmed by the hand of Poqanghoya, while Palongawhoya sounded his call and all the vibratory centers along the earth's axis resounded. "The whole earth trembled; the universe quivered in tune." The whole world became attuned, resounding the praise of the Creator.

When their special work was completed they were sent, one to the south pole and the other to the north pole, to keep the earth rotating in an established harmony, or rhythm. One was instructed to keep the earth solid and firm while the other was assigned to keep the air in gentle motion and to send out his call for good or for warning. These duties looked toward the future because creation had not yet fully been accomplished.

Now the Spider Woman set about the creation of the world of nature: trees, plants, bushes, each with its own name and order of life. Then followed birds of all kinds and animals, each one in its own line of life, with its own peculiar or special name. She covered each with the substance of her white-mantled cape, which they would share in the wisdom of the Creator. "Some she placed to her right, some to her left; others before and behind her, indicating how they should spread to all four corners of the earth to live."

When Taiowa saw what she had done he was well pleased and said, "It is ready now for human life, the final touch to complete my plan."

At this point we may observe that the intent of the Creator in readying the world for man was to establish order and harmony. These were built into the very fabric of creation. One is reminded of an experience of Admiral Byrd at the South Pole when he was alone, quite removed from the camp base. He stood outside his hut and seemed to *hear* the harmony of creation in the vast quiet of the Antarctic twilight.

The day was dying, the night being born—but with great peace. Here were the imponderable processes and forces of the cosmos, harmonious and soundless. Harmony, that was it! That was what came out of the silence —a gentle rhythm, the strain of a perfect chord, the music of the spheres, perhaps.

It was enough to catch that rhythm, momentarily to be myself a part of it. In that instant I could feel no doubt of man's oneness with the universe. The conviction came that that rhythm was too orderly, too harmonious, too perfect to be a product of blind chance—that, therefore, there must be purpose in the whole and that man was part of that whole and not an accidental offshoot. It was a feeling that transcended reason; that went to the heart of man's despair and found it groundless. The universe was a cosmos, not a chaos; man was as rightfully a part of that cosmos as were the day and night.

Is this the prelude to what the poet saw when he says, referring to man, "Grand as the rest may be, he ruins it?" We shall see.

In the creation of mankind, Spider Woman followed the same general procedure as before, except that she chose four colors of earth: yellow, red, white, and black. She mixed the earth with saliva, molded it into shapes, then covered them with the white substance of her cape, creative wisdom itself. The first four men were made in the image of Sotuknang, after which she created four other human beings in her image to be their partners. When they were all uncovered they came to life, but not until the mantle of creative wisdom had done its work in them. When the mantle was lifted, they were alive. This was the time of the dark purple light, the first phase of the dawn of creation "which first reveals the mystery of man's creation."

When they first awoke and began to move, their foreheads were damp and a soft spot was in the crown of their heads. This marked the second phase of the creation of man, the time of the yellow light, for it was now that the breath of life entered man.

Then the sun appeared to dry them off and to harden the soft spot in their heads—this to mark the time of the yellow light as the third phase of the dawn of creation. Man, now fully formed, was ready to face his Creator, fashioned in His image.

The Spider Woman said to them: "That is the Sun. You are meeting your Father the Creator for the first time. You must always remember and observe the three phases of your Creation. The time of the three lights, the dark purple, the yellow, and the red, reveal in turn the mystery, the breath of life, and the warmth of love. These comprise the Creator's *plan* of life for you as sung over you in the Song of Creation." This was the time of the red light.

Because they had not been given the power of speech, the First People of the First World could not answer her. So Sotuknang was summoned. The Spider Woman said to him, "As you commanded me, I have created these First People. They are fully and firmly formed; they are properly colored; they have life; they have movement. But they cannot talk. . . . So I want you to give them speech. Also the wisdom and the power to reproduce, so that they may enjoy their life and give thanks to the Creator."

It was done. A different language was given to each color. They were given the wisdom and the power to reproduce and multiply.

Then Sotuknang said to them, "With all these I have given you this world to live on and to be happy. There is only one thing I ask of you—to respect the Creator at all times. Wisdom, *harmony* (community), and respect for the love of the Creator who made you, may it grow and never be forgotten among you as long as you live."

In their happiness the First People began to multiply.

The nature of man, as conceived in the Hopi creation myth, clearly illustrates my basic thesis concerning order, harmony, and actualized potential as reflected in the racial memory of a "forgotten harmony." As a result of the work of the mantle of wisdom, which was central to the process of creation, man knew that the earth was a living entity like himself. The earth itself was alive and living. The Creator breathed through the earth. Such is the experience of many persons, even in our time, who live close to the earth. It seems to be alive—not merely vital but alive! The Hopi idea was that those created in the First World knew that they were made from the flesh of the earth and were nourished at her breast. The grass upon which all animals fed was the milk of her body. To them, the corn plant was also a living entity with a body very much like their own. It was a simple step to make—Earth Mother, Corn Mother.

They knew their father also in two dimensions. First, as we have seen, they knew him as the Sun. This is not difficult to understand or appreciate, for the sun, the great source of life, was not known to them until he appeared at the time of the red light. In the second dimension they were aware that the sun was but the face through which looked Taiowa, their Creator. Always they felt themselves to be in immediate and primary relationship with the universal entities out of which they had come—their human parts were merely channels through which the Creator created.

The myth goes into minute detail concerning the revealing sacramental character of the dedicatory ceremony, from the time of the birth of a child to that climactic moment when the mother is able to step forward, presenting her child to the rising sun with these words: "Father Sun, this is your child."

The Hopi child's first seven or eight years are carefree and full of vital irresponsibility. Then he must take an active part in the religious aspect of the common life. He must now learn that despite the fact of his having human parents, his true parents are the universal entities of which in some real sense his parents are but symbols —Mother Earth and Father Sun. All flesh comes from the former and all life from the latter. Always he participates in the very essence of these two universals. He finds also that there are two dimensions within himself. He is a member of an earthly family and clan, and he is, as well, a citizen of the universe. A more modern way of saying this is that he is both a space-binder and a time-binder. These First People sensed the mystery of their own parenthood as well as their own structure and nature.

The myth seeks to interpret or account for the way in which the intent of the Creator could make itself manifest in the behavior of the First People. On various parts of the body were openings. At the top of the head was the "open door" through which "he received his life and connected with his Creator." During the last phase of creation this soft spot was hardened; the door was closed, not to be opened until the time of death, when he departed from his body even as he had entered.

The most exciting development in the account describes the second center, the brain, just beneath the soft spot. It is with this organ, this part of himself, that he learned to think about himself, the world, and how he was to function in it. According to the myth, the real function of the thinking organ was to discover the intent, the plan, of the Creator.

The third center was the throat, through which he received the breath of life and through which he was able to give back his breath in sound. More and more as he became acquainted with himself he used this center to give praise to his Creator.

The fourth center was the organ that pulsated with the vibration of life itself, the heart. Here was the center of feeling, in which he experienced the good of life so long as he was of one heart; but when evil feelings entered he became of two hearts. It is in this center that he *sensed* the purpose of life.

Finally, there was the fifth center, the solar plexus—the throne in man that was occupied by the Creator, and from whence he directed all the life of man.

The First People were one in body and mind; therefore they did not know sickness. Sickness came only when the inner community of body and mind was disrupted by evil. The people were pure, innocent, and happy. The same quality obtains here as in the Garden of Eden. The people multiplied and grew, covering the face of the land. *Despite the fact that they were of different colors and spoke different languages, they were one people and understood one another without speech or talking. The same was true of the birds and animals. Different forms there were, but there was one life, nourished by Mother Earth and sired and sustained by the Sun, through which the Creator worked or created.*

In time, the First People forgot the original command to respect the Creator as the condition of their creation and continuity. More and more they forsook His plan and intent that the people and the animals should all be one. Simultaneous with their estrangement from the plan of Creation, there came among them the Talker, in the form of a bird called Mochni. He kept talking among them, always making the same point that the people and the animals were fundamentally different and that the same was true of the people whose colors and languages varied. Accordingly, the differences were absolute and made a true distinction between peoples and between people and animals.

Differences now became not merely apparent but dramatic. The animals began to draw away from man, and men began drawing away from one another. Fear, the great enemy of community, appeared. The final separation among the people was between those who remembered the plan and intent of the Creator and those who did not.

It is unnecessary to follow the fate of the Hopis through all the experiences of new creations and fresh starts, including the final or Fourth World. The common thread remains: creation with the harmony of innocence, the loss of innocence with a disintegration of the harmony. Waters' summary will suffice:

Man is created perfect in the image of his Creator. Then after "closing the door," "falling from grace" into the uninhibited expression of his own human will, he begins his slow climb back upward. Within him are several psychological centers. At each successive stage of his evolution one of these comes into dominant play. Also for each stage there is created a world-body in the same order of development as his own body, for him to become manifest upon. When each successive period of development concludes with catastrophic destruction to the world and mankind, he passes on to the next. . . . In the fourth stage of development he reaches the lowest and midpoint of his journey. The Fourth World, the present one, is the full expression of man's ruthless materialism and imperialistic will; and man himself reflects the gross appetites of the flesh. With this turn man rises upward, bringing into predominant function each of the higher centers. The door at the crown of the head then opens, and he merges into the *wholeness* of all Creation, whence he sprang. It is a Road of Life he has traveled by his own free will, exhausting every capacity for good or evil, that he may know himself at last as a finite part of infinity.

This creation myth repeats the primordial theme that dramatizes the ancient hunger of the spirit of man for a spiritual order that is never quite completely his but is an integral part of a reality that nourishes in him the "memory of a lost harmony," a memory latent in the soul and not distilled from the changing things of mere physical observation. In this way the inner unity of the known and the knower may be preserved, and the almost mythic intuition of reality thereby related to its conceptual and rational forms of expression.

Here, as in Genesis, community (wholeness) is given to illustrate the intent of the Creator in creation. It is as if a model of community is provided that man might know the meaning of life. He has the potential that may be actualized in him as the fulfillment of the intent of the Creator. But it must be pointed out also that man has the potential for the rejection of the intent of the Creator. But the Creator is insistent that ultimately his intent will not be defeated. And this becomes at once the hope for both man and the Creator. The racial memory troubles man's sleep and grieves his waking hours, making him dream of peace even in the midst of war.

In these two creation accounts, the starting point for man on earth is a situation that is orderly, whole, complete, integrated—a climate of community. This is the great racial assumption about the origin of man and the living context in which he is to grow, develop, and multiply. The *experience* of the race, however, at any moment in time, is an acute awareness of the absence of harmony. How can the cruel vicissitudes of disharmony, discord, disorder be tolerated without a sense of ultimate despair? There floats from the dim region of ancient memory the racial assurance that this condition is not normal, but the result of something "other" that has been set forth and established. (Interestingly enough, there is no effort to attempt to explain the original fact of community, except that it is a part of the givenness of the creative act.) There was a time —the experience of life was whole and continuity obtained through and in all its manifestations. It was when life was fresh from the mind of the Creator or from the womb of the earth that it was untarnished and innocent. This was given by the Creator as the already actualized potential, as if the Creator wanted man to know what his true intent was in bringing life into being, and this experience of true intent was to serve as a constant tutor, reminding man in the midst of all of his divisions, chaos, disorder, and broken harmony that he was made in and for harmony. Thus man would never accept the absence of community as his destiny. When he asks, then, what life was like before there was pain, hate, bitterness, and violence, the word comes back that life was beautiful and whole, tranquil and full of peace. Man has lost this dimension in his journey; he has sinned and missed the way, so these accounts remind us; but the echo, the sound of harmony, has not died in his dream. It lives in his myths, and what he hears in the echo is at times more real than the distortions through which he passes in his day-by-day endeavor. Again, the important clue to the Creator's intent is to be found in the racial memory of what life was like when life began.

The experience of community as man's *actualized* potential must be distinguished from the experience of community as potential.

The experience of community as instant fact is the experience of innocence. These myths show clearly that the potential for disharmony also resides in man. Mark you, both good and evil are potential, but the accounts take pains to explain that the sample that man is permitted to experience as explicit in his creation is community, the good. The potential for disharmony is triggered by his exercise of choice, by volition, in which he commits himself to the choice. Once this is done, he is no longer innocent. Once man has embarked upon his journey, these two potentials exist in him as parallel lines that cannot merge. It is not until he *achieves* goodness that they may blend into creative synthesis. Man's original experience of community is both potential and actualized potential within the framework of innocence. During this period the things that work against community are dormant. The experience of community based upon innocence obtains so long as elements of disharmony are not apparent. There is present the freedom and abandonment of innocence, and yet the freedom is not absolute. Freedom has meaning only with reference to limitations in some form. The fact that Adam and Eve were not permitted to eat the fruit of the tree of knowledge gave meaning to the experience of freedom. They also lacked responsibility in all aspects of their life except with reference to eating the forbidden fruit. Where there is prohibition, there is cost or penalty; hence responsibility is inevitable.

Responsibility operates at two levels where actions are concerned. There is the responsibility that flows automatically from the act itself, which sets in motion elements that are dormant prior to the act. By his act the individual precipitates a chain reaction before which he may be helpless and by which he is carried on to the conclusion of the logic of the act itself.

In the story of the Garden of Eden, Adam's act was of that kind, as were the acts of the First People in the First World of the Hopi. A whole series of events followed, in both instances, throughout the world of nature and beyond, which were not viable until the crucial act or acts were performed. In this sense the responsibility for the act is impersonal. Secondly, there is also a profound element of personal responsibility here. This is shown initially by Adam. He feels guilty, he realizes that he is naked, he is ashamed. Something in him is broken down and he is no longer at peace. He accuses the woman, he hides from God, and his whole world is thrown out of harmony. He is faced with the responsibility for his action. But it does not stop there. The story continues:

> Then the Lord God said to the woman,
> "What have you done?" The woman said,
> "It was the serpent that misled me, so I ate it." So the Lord God said to the serpent,
> "Because you have done this, the most cursed of all *animals* shall you be, and of all the wild beasts. On your belly you shall crawl, and eat dust, as long as you live. I will put enmity between you and the world, and between your posterity and hers; they shall attack you in the head, and you shall attack them in the heel." To the woman he said,
> "I will make your pain at childbirth very great; in pain shall you bear children; and yet you shall be devoted to your husband, while he shall rule over you." And to the man he said,
> "Because you followed your wife's suggestions, and ate from the tree from which I commanded you not to eat,
> "Cursed shall be the ground through you,
> "In suffering shall you gain your living from it as long as you live;
> "Thorns and thistles shall it produce for you, so that you will have to eat wild plants,
> "By the sweat of your brow shall you earn your living, until you return to the ground,
> "Since it was from it that you were taken; for dust you are, and to dust you must return."

When through a responsible act on his part, an act of deliberate choice, that which is dormant and therefore potential becomes active or becomes actualized potential, then the two parallel lines merge in him and a sense of guilt becomes his portion. This guilt has to be purged before he can triumph in goodness. What is meant here can best be understood by examining the difference between goodness and innocence. That which is innocent is essentially untried, untested, unchallenged. It is complete and whole in itself because it has known nothing else. When innocence is lost because of violation, however defined, something in the individual begins working to recover a lost grace. When the *quality* of goodness has been reestablished, a great change has taken place. Eyes are opened, knowledge is defined, and what results is the triumph of the quality of innocence over the quality of discord; a new synthesis is achieved that has in it the element of triumph. That is, a child is innocent, but a man who has learned how to winnow beauty out of ugliness, purity out of stain, tranquility out of tempest, joy out of sorrow, life out of death—only such a man may be said to be good. But he is no longer innocent.

Man was put out of the Garden of Eden with his innocence lost, his sense of community within himself and with all of life corrupted, the victim of guilt and struggle, with all the tempests that revolve around the head of the tortured spirit. The judgment is very solemn. "Therefore the Lord God sent him from the Garden of Eden, to till the ground from whence he was taken. So he drove out the man; and he placed at the east of the Garden of Eden Cherubim, and a flaming sword which turned every way to keep the way of the tree of life."

In like manner the First People of the Hopi myth were sent forth on the Road of Life to wander and struggle and suffer until they came to their own place—until they came home to themselves, until they became whole.

The story of man's struggle on the planet, haunting him as he builds his cultures, his civilizations, as he erects his altars and makes his sacrifices before his God, is to find his way back to the Garden of Eden, which must yet be achieved. To achieve community in the midst of all the things he brought upon himself by his own deeds, things that work most against community, is to sweep past the angel with the flaming sword and build a new home in the Garden of Eden. At man's moments of greatest despair he is instinctively unwilling and perhaps unable to accept the contradictions of his life as final or ultimate. Something deep within reminds him that the intent of the Creator of life and the living substance is that men must live in harmony within themselves and with one another and perhaps with all of life. When he seeks to achieve it, even in his little world of belonging and meaning, what is at first the dim racial memory stirring deep within him becomes the paean of a great transcendent chorus rejoicing him on his way.

It may be that man's experience of himself as a child of nature and the long journey of his organism to self-consciousness and reflective thought may yield another clue to what seems to be the ground of community in the integrity of life itself.

III

The Search in Living Structures

It is in order to explore the meaning of man's experience of community both as a child of nature and as a kinsman of all living things. For the purpose of our discussion, life is viewed in at least two very basic dimensions. The first is life in the sense of existence, of process, of manifestation—indeed, of energy itself. Here life is thought of as creation, as a vast all-pervasive quality with an infinite number of configurations and forms. Considered in this way, we think of life without particular consciousness as we experience it or know it, but rather as rhythmic movement, as ebb and flow, as integration and disintegration, as orderliness and disorderliness. In such a view, the notion of beginning and ending has no meaning. Life simply *is*.

When the notion of beginning is introduced into this view of life, the mind comes up against a dead end because there is nowhere for *before* to locate itself as an idea in the mind. Hence, in terms of this dimension of life, such words as origin or starting place are meaningless, but they are by no means without value as a necessity of thought. For religion, the creation accounts, myths, or query stories respond to such a necessity; for science, the creation hypotheses undertake the same assignment. The difference, however, is that the latter may be a deduction from a series of interpretations of observation and very limited experimentation, which deduction may give to the investigation of the external world considerable substance and meaning. In terms of human life and its meaning in the total enterprise, the creation myths may prove just as fruitful.

Let us now spell out briefly what seems to be a gathered meaning of life in this first dimension. What confronts us at once is the unbelievable immensity of the universe in time and space. Modern studies of the universe deal with cosmic processes rather than with a fixed and therefore limited universe. When I was a boy I regarded the stars as fixed, stationary objects in the sky *above;* in fact, there was a period when I thought they were peepholes through which God looked down upon the world. The vast cosmic processes gather in their sweep not only energy transfers and transformations that alter the form and the shapes of units in the universe, but also the progressive or evolutionary changes in the universe as well. Such processes account for the origin and flux of matter itself. In a word, it seems that such processes are in part observed to be expressions of meaningful patterns or constructs. It would seem that although the stars are infinite in number, the *kinds* of stars are relatively few—that stars change with time. They are of a certain characteristic when they originate. These characteristics change over long periods of time until the stars come to an end, scattering their matter and energy back into the universe as a whole. Of such is the background of life on our earth, and from this process we are assured that all the energy and matter that go into the making of living things on the earth were created, and eligible niches for life were provided.

Life in accordance with this first dimension seems to be realizing itself in the all-inclusive immensity of the universe. It seems to be living itself out, and in so doing, there seem to be discernible patterns, areas of structured relations that provide observable stability. Of course, the moment such terms as patterns and structures are used, the mind thinks in terms of organization of some kind. And organization suggests plan, design, purpose. But the use of the term "life" in this first dimension presents a view of organization without the correlative notion of active consciousness. According to this view, there are agencies or forces, such as energy, magnetic fields, and the work horse of the concept: stimulus and response. There are such elements of the "given" called properties, energized particles, and so forth. In all of this thought the one idea seems to be to rid the mind of the necessity for positing a First Cause, a Creator, a supernatural Being, without at the same time undermining the concept of order, behavior, and integration in that part of the natural world in which mind as we know it is not actively present. Every effort is made to make even such a term as immanence unnecessary because its twin, transcendence, might slip by unnoticed.

Nevertheless, recent investigations confirm the notion that the universe is a *universe*. There seems to be a vast, almost incomprehensible interrelatedness tying all together. As Lawrence Frank suggests in his *Nature and Human Nature:*

Nature is both stable and orderly but also plastic and flexible, capable of entering new patterns and diversified combinations, as we see in the variety of structures and organisms of the geographical environment. But even these varied forms and products have not exhausted the possibilities and potentialities. . . . On each level of organization different possibilities appear as the constituent parts, by their interaction organize into new configurations in which constituents *behave* differently as they participate in a different organization or field.

Further he adds:

Every single electron, every single emission or radiation of energy, as well as every atom, molecule or larger configuration is, therefore, resonating in its field, actively participating in maintaining and operating a larger configuration and, thus, the universe.

The universe is now conceived, not as some tidy little restricted collection of planets and their sun, governed by arbitrary power or deterministic forces, but as a space-time manifold of almost unbelievable magnitude and a history going back towards, but never reaching, a beginning and a future of unlimited time, with a capacity for self-regulation and self-direction.

Perhaps it is merely a limitation of language, but it seems to me significant that the latter terms are value judgments relating to consciousness.

Since we are not only living in the universe but the universe is living in us, it follows, then, that man is an organic part of the universe. In his organism he experiences the order and harmony of the universe. In fact, it would not have been possible for him to emerge had certain conditions not been maintained so that life for him and all his multitudinous kinsmen could be sustained.

We come now to what seem to be the most incredible manifestations of directiveness on the part of life in the aspect under discussion, namely, the establishing of precise conditions for the existence and maintenance of life on earth. There are at least two facts that must be taken into account at the outset. The first is that the background of life in its second dimension (consciousness, awareness, irritability) cannot be separated from the functioning of life in its first dimension. The activity of stars, of which our sun is a minor one, involves the condensation of primordial matter into the configurations of atoms, which configurations are indissolubly involved in the substance of all living organisms. And stellar activity provides the planetary platform for the development of organisms.

The second incredible manifestation of apparent directiveness is the fact that life on earth is very restricted in its territory of occupancy. It is confined to a thin shell that includes uniquely the interfaces among land, air, and water. It seems that life cannot exist very far down in the land masses, nor very high in the atmosphere, nor in the abyss of the oceans (except in a very limited way). "Life's habitat," states Clifford Grobstein, "is the relatively thin zone where land, sea, and sky meet." The technical term is biosphere. This extraordinary phenomenon is but another expression of the order mechanism by means of which life "knows" what it must do in order to realize itself, its limitations and boundaries in which it actualizes its potential or experiences community. The basis for this behavior is in the fact that the energetic foundation of all life is converted solar energy—"the radiated output of thermonuclear fusion in the core of the sun," states Grobstein. Hence light is crucial to maintenance of life. This fact is a part of the practical knowledge of all who have had any experience with growing things. But the light is filtered through a kind of protective covering surrounding the earth that admits so-called cosmic rays from the sun in what may be regarded as nonlethal or broken doses. Again, life is not equally distributed everywhere in the biosphere or in the zone where land, sea, and sky meet. The total quantity of material making up the living organisms in any given area within the habitable zone is called biomass. The total biomass on the planet has never and perhaps can never be measured. Within the biomass it is crucial to my thesis to point out that here also order, organization, is characteristic of "behavior." Again Grobstein: "A fundamental property of the biomass is its organization into assemblages of different kinds of units—groups or organisms that exist in characteristic associations with each other and with their environment." Such associations are seen as functional groupings essential to what is going on in the whole biomass and its component organisms. Such a secondary characteristic is called ecosystem.

Thus the universe is not only vast and overwhelming in its immensity, it is also minutely structured and coordinated, maintaining itself by a boundless energy that configurates in rich variety, each configuration integrated with other units to comprise the totality of the universe. There are systems within systems within systems, all held together and contained by a "boundless" boundlessness. There are apparently no fixed limits within the sweep of the universe, only a cumulative heterogeneity held together by the relative stability of relationships through the dynamic characteristics of a kind of magnetic field or series of fields.

The point at which the second dimension of life becomes evident is at a blending of or fading from one into the other. In other words, there are no apparent signposts marking the point in time and space at which the inanimate becomes animate.

It is in the life of the organism that the meaning of community within our definition takes on its most fruitful significance. We begin, then, with the way life functions in the areas of concentration where living organisms are to be found. These areas depend upon the use of energy from the sun. Not all of the components within a given area can capture this energy. Those that are able to take their energy neat are self-nourishing in the presence of light. They live on light and simple organic substances, which they convert for nourishment and which in part they cast off as enriched decomposition. Such self-nourishing organisms are mainly green plants, which make up one large component of all living organisms.

A second kind of organism must secure its solar energy in a secondary manner by consuming components of the first classification. These are animals that feed on green plants that take their solar energy directly and build up new complex compounds essential to their own needs. In this process of nourishment they release smaller molecules that are crucial raw materials for the things upon which they feed. Thus we see a basic cycle of energy and materials that sustains the total life in the given area. Here is a fleeting glimpse of the dynamic nature of the life within any given area of the biomass. There are many such systems and each has a metabolism of its own. The potential in any given expression of life is actualized and becomes involved in this very process in the actualizing of the potential of some other form of life upon which it is dependent. The cycle is endless, and the integration of any form cannot be thought of as independent of a similar process in other forms. Here is structural dependency expressive of an exquisite harmony—the very genius of the concept of community. There is a constant and flowing interaction between the organism and the larger environment, and each change in the environment is reflected in the organism. In fact, it seems very difficult to make a clear distinction between the external and internal environment of the organism.

Studies in the field make the point that there is within the internal environment a highly sensitive system of communication. The chief agent is blood, with its network of channels through which it flows throughout the body. In its continuous movement from the heart through the arteries and veins, it is burdened with traffic to and from the various organs. It filters selectively from the lungs and the intestines that which will be taken out, absorbed, or eliminated at some other point along its circulatory journey. The wonder is that the blood is kept stable by the activities of the various organs within the system. It is dependent, for instance, upon the lungs, kidneys, and liver for its basic regulation, while at the same time it carries to these organs what is crucial to their own peace. Here is the operation of complex, intricate, patterned behavior as if it were committed to memory at some far-off time in an unknowable past.

Inasmuch as all the bodily cells are sustained by the nourishment received from their geographical environment, those cells that are deep within the body could not live without the life-giving food supplied by the bloodstream. It is through the work of the red cells that oxygen is supplied to those organs that need it for survival or sustenance.

When we take a cursory view of the white cells, for instance, we see them functioning primarily as scavengers, maintaining the integrity of the bloodstream and the tissues. They are the defenders of the faith, as it were. Some of the very specialized cells of the body have apparently lost their primitive capacity of self-defense and must rely upon the bloodstream for their protection. Communication and protection are characteristic functions of the bloodstream in order that the harmony of the organism may be maintained and its potential may be actualized through organic development, fulfillment, and death.

Just as crucial to the process of system-maintenace is the function of blood plasma. Its different elements and specific functions hold in critical balance a dynamic reserve of what is needed by different parts of the organism for nourishment and protection. The sensitivity that makes for immunity against certain diseases and the recurrence of others; the provision of essential chemicals in steady supply or upon special demand; the stabilizing of the internal environment of the organism by balancing its own constituents, by drawing upon the stored reserves or by stimulating various organic systems to decrease or increase activity and to supply more or eliminate any excess through well-defined channels of elimination —all these are part of the magical power or orderly function of the blood plasma.

The lymphatic system may be called a secondary channel of communication. In this system fluids circulate among the different tissues and organs, making available under systemic duress additional white cells at times of emergency within the organism. It keeps the different internal functions interrelated and coordinated. Within the lymphatic system there are special pockets or reservoirs called nodes, where the invaders in the organisms are isolated and destroyed by the white cell militia of the body. It is to be noted that a certain kind of discrimination in function may be lacking, because under certain conditions the lymphatic system may distribute infections and malignancies as well.

The uncanny devices, mechanisms, processes, or characteristics within the human body by which health and immunity to hostile invasion are maintained seem to express behavior that is not a part of the self-conscious activity of the organism as such. In other words, it does not seem to be related to the function of the mind as we know it. There is something in the body itself that recognizes proteins of other living organisms as strangers and that is capable of organizing and carrying out an attack against them. If they cannot be destroyed, they must be incarcerated in some way until they can be ejected or their danger neutralized. The power to recognize and destroy such invaders is called immunity. It is a highly organized defense system and proves itself in combat every day in the lives of both human beings and animals.

When an invasion occurs on a small scale by a scouting party of proteins, the defenses throw them out. If it happens again, there is justly accentuated opposition, and the possibility of a disease developing from the activity of the invaders is reduced and often not possible. It is curious that the defense mechanism seems to "remember," and as long as the memory is active, immunity against the disease is the result.

In Dr. Francis D. Moore's discussion of tissue transplantation as it was developed at the Peter Bent Brigham Hospital in Boston, a teaching facility affiliated with the Harvard Medical School, he makes the point that the immunity process has two leading components: the antigen and the antibody. The antigen generates antagonism—it is the substance that exerts an immune response, and it is usually a protein. When an antigen gains entrance into the body it calls forth specific antagonists, the antibodies. These are also proteins and are manufactured by special tissues that are devoted to the process of immunity. The antibodies, together with a substance called "complement," immobilize the invading protein antigen, thus preparing it for disposal or elimination.

An awareness of the battle that may be raging against the invaders is often evidenced in the organism by a rise in temperature and a feeling of discomfort. If the antibodies win, peace is restored, the lost harmony is recovered. If they lose, the organism dies. But there is a third possibility or alternative: the antigen may be permitted to remain in the organism without being molested. In other words, the antigen may be tolerated for "good behavior."

In the transplanting of tissues from one body to the other, it is apparent that the transplanted tissues must contain antigens that are resisted by the host body. This is true notwithstanding the fact that the new tissue will possibly save the life of its new host. The mechanism of defense that guarantees immunity against invasion is automatic, and it is impossible for the body to decide when and under what circumstances to resist invasion on grounds that are secured by the behavior pattern of the organism itself. The most effective way to achieve this is by making it temporarily impossible for the new host to make antibodies, thus rendering it defenseless until such time as the transplant can become established, making defensive resistence unnecessary. This has been accomplished first with X rays and subsequently with certain drugs. The only point of relevance here is that the immunity system seems to operate on the basis of what in human behavior would be called recognition, tolerance, and memory. One cannot escape the thought that all kinds of precautions have developed within organisms to keep their relationship with the internal environment in harmony with the external geographic environment, so that life may realize itself without hindrance in a given form, thereby experiencing wholeness, integration, community within the tight circle of its particular existence. Such an achievement never takes place *in vacuo.*

The major channel of communication for synchronizing the wide variety of internal active processes in the organism and for keeping it in vital and constant touch with the external environment is the nervous system. Here we see a series of highly specialized cells functioning in ways that result from slow changes that have taken place over millions of years. In addition, there is a vast network of nerve fibers consisting of many subnetworks and subsidiary patterns. In fact, the nervous system is a delicately fashioned, interlocking directorate of immense flexibility and responsiveness. It is an amazing achievement in creative artistry and efficiency. Suffice it to say that, putting aside temporarily the concept of mind as synonymous with self-consciousness, the nervous system as a responsive structure within the organism is firmly established as a going concern that coordinates, dispatches, transposes, and crossfiles messages that keep the organism in constant correspondence with its external environment so as to guarantee and perpetuate, to the limit, the life of the individual and, beyond this, to safeguard the continuity of biological organization to which the organism belongs.

It is not to be wondered at that the concept of directiveness of organic activities seems to be so plausible. If we began with such a complex structure as the human nervous system and moved backward in time as far as its development is concerned, we would become involved with subtle interwoven and interdependent structures of varied kinds and functions, until we landed inside the minutely balanced intricacies of the single cells of the human body. Within these cells we would come upon those invisible configurations of energy that inform the cell of its goals and directions, determining a future concerning which it has no awareness but about which it has absolute confidence. The farther the search is carried on the more we seem to be moving into the ground of a reality that shapes and reshapes itself, is self-perpetuating in its vitality, and makes its rules of function out of the tensions created by a hidden intent brought to bear upon a recalcitrant but responsive environment. In short, the organism seems to be a self-maintaining, reproducing, developing whole. Man's experience as a creature is that of an alternating rhythm between his internal environment and the external, geographical environment by which he is nurtured and sustained. When, for any reason, this rhythm is broken through the malfunctioning of any of his organic parts, then automatically, often without his leave, processes are set in motion for the restoration of the orderly process of unself-conscious respiration, or health.

Indeed, a man becomes aware of any particular part of his organism only when it is malfunctioning. He regards himself as being ill or sick when at some point his organism is maladjusted. Therapy, or healing, is an effort to restore the organism to harmony and to rhythm. A continuous wearing away or breaking down of the organism and a continuous repairing and rebuilding—the processes of renewal and repair are an integral part of the basic mechanism of the organism itself. Its resourcefulness in this regard is beyond accurate calculation. But even here there are limits, because it is an organism and its dwelling place is in that relatively limited area of the planet where land, sea, and sky meet. Despite the precariousness of life for the organism, its every move is marked by a structure-functional integrity, so that activities essential to life can be carried on in a coordinated and integrated way. The *intent* is for integration, for wholeness, for community within the limitations of the organism itself.

In speaking of the wondrous interactions of the human body, Sir

Charles Sherrington begins by saying that the human child has at birth twenty-six million cells. Continuing, he says:

They have arranged themselves in a complex, which is a human child. Each cell in all that more than millionfold population has taken up its right position. Each has assumed its required form and size in the right place. The whole is not merely specific but is a particular individual within the specific.

In that individual, that "persona," each cell has taken on the shape which will suit its particular business in the cell-community of which it is a member, whether its skill is to lie in mechanical pulling, chemical manufacture, gas-transport, radiation-absorption, or what not. More still, it has done so as though it "knew" the minute local conditions of the particular spot in which its lot is cast. It knows not "up" from "down"; it works in the dark. Yet the nerve cell, for instance, "finds" even to the finger tips the nerve cell with which it should touch fingers. It is as if an immanent principle inspired each cell with knowledge for carrying out of a design. And this picture which the microscope supplies to us, supplies us after all, because it is but a picture, with only the static form. That is but the outward and visible sign of a dynamic activity, which is a harmony in time as well as space.

Concerning differentiating cells in development, Sherrington says:

They, as the case may require, pour out cement which binds, or fluid in which they shall move free; or they hold hands for surer and more sensitive contact. Some will have changed their stuff and become rigid bone, or, harder still, the enamel of a tooth; some become fluid as water so as to flow along tubes too fine for the eye to see. Some become clear as glass, some opaque as stone, some colourless, some red, some black. Some become factories of a furious chemistry, some become as inert as death. Some become engines of mechanical pull, some scaffoldings of static support. Each one of all the millions upon millions finally specializes in something helpful to the whole. . . . It is as if the life of each one of all those millions has understood its special part. Thus arises the new integral individual to be.

This summary of man's experience of his creaturehood suggests that man is in a very real sense one of the products of time-bound evolutionary processes exhibiting characteristics that we associate with the activity of mind: direction and purpose. The very existence of mind in man may be but an expression of man's total response to the history of his organism. But once the existence of mind became possible and therefore a part of the reality of man's experience of the world and of himself, the way was open for him to do directly and deliberately and purposefully what nature has done through eons of time and with much trial and error. It may be that the meaning of his experience will bear its richest fruits only when his brain is more fully developed, thus tying his future inextricably into the ground of his creaturehood. It is not unreasonable, then, to assume that as he seeks community within himself, with his fellows, and with his world, he may find that what he is seeking to do deliberately is but the logic of the meaning of all that has gone into his own creation.

I believe that God stands in relation to all existence somewhat as the mind in man stands in relation to his time-space existence.

We turn now to examine how our thesis applies to man's dreams and anticipations of his possible future as expressed in his projections called Utopias.

IV

The Search in The Prophet's Dream

There seems to be an intimate connection between the view of life as seen through the symbolism of the creation myths and the dream of the future as seen through the eyes of the prophet, the seer, and the Utopian. One is hidden deep within the mystery of an unrecorded past, the articulation of a primordial stirring in the human spirit; the other is a projection into a chartless future, in which the power of the imagination and the reflections of the mind can move freely within a predetermined structure. In the myth, the created world existed first in the formlessness of chaos or in the mind of the gods or god; in the Utopias, the created worlds were fashioned out of elements in the heart and yearnings of men who were part of the times in which they lived.

Utopia's most pronounced characteristic is a limited and contained community in which the potential of the individual as well as that of the society can be actualized. Every element is defined in a manner that makes its presence identical with its function. In other words, Utopias are custom made, even though men must live in them. It is as if an entire society and physical environment were fashioned to order. Ever since men began to reflect upon the meaning of their own lives and experiences and to set them down in written form, the dream of what life could be *if* has occupied a significant place in their calculations. Community as it is experienced in the far-flung hopes of men in all ages finds its greatest fulfillment in a picture of what the collective life of man would be like if it functioned in keeping with man's high destiny. Man "has continued to dream ever of a better world, to speculate as to its possible nature, and to communicate his longings to other men in the hope that the ideal might, at least in part, become reality." The form and the character of the images vary in accordance not only with the private hopes and frustrations of the dreamer but also in accordance with the idealized social form of the particular period in which the dreamer lived.

As mentioned earlier, man has an inner and an outer environment. What is true of man as a biological creature is also true of him as a person. He has an inner world of meaning, feelings, aspirations, that has its own particular reality. As Jane Steger suggests: "The inner life may be as full of adventure, explorations, hopes and fears, and 'perilous seas,' as the outer life. . . . There is a wide other world within, deep harbors of thought, marvelous seas of contemplation, waiting to be explored." In times of great stress and strain in the outer environment, men tend to retreat or escape into the inner world as a place of shelter or refuge. In some cases, retreat is an end in itself; in others, men turn to the inner environment, bringing with them the articulate urgency to build out of their imagination a way of life, a world order that has no time or place in the present but can be released as something that, if its power were absolute, would come to pass somewhere, sometime. Having been released from the binding stricture of the present circumstance, they can build whole new worlds full of all that is lacking in their present experience. In this sense, Utopias may be regarded as mechanisms of escape for those who are not hardy enough to cope with the issues and vicissitudes of life as it must be lived.

But this is not the whole picture by any means. Any review of

Utopian literature shows that often Utopias of one age are geared to the basic structure of that period and point the way to a fresh possibility for mankind in the arduous struggle to actualize its own potential—if not now, then hereafter. But the hereafter is in the world, not in the heavens.

Lewis Mumford makes the interesting distinction between Utopias that are places of refuge for the spirit and those that undertake to project a place of release at some time in the future. The former he calls Utopias of escape, the latter Utopias of reconstruction. "The first leaves the external world the way it is; the second seeks to change it so that one may have intercourse with it in one's own terms. In one we build impossible castles in the air; in the other we consult a surveyor and an architect and a mason and proceed to build a house which meets our essential needs; as well as houses made of stone and mortar are capable of meeting them."

Utopias are rooted in the very structure of man's conscious life. There is a spirit that hovers over all the generations of man that rejects the contradictions of his private and social life as being either ultimate or final. It refuses to accept the idea that life as it is being lived is meaningless. If the meaning that a man seeks cannot be a part of the present fact, if the testing of his current experience can make room only for the positive and destructive, then he projects himself beyond the present into the future, which holds securely against the vicissitudes of the present. Of course, for the individual this may easily be expressed in a kind of wishful thinking, the spiraling overtones of a mind unable to deal with the realities of its literal experience, but this is not the whole story by far. Over against all of the discontinuity of any age, continuity always presses and never yields. Even when men are sure that what they seek is a dream that can never be realized in their lifetime or in the lifetime of all who live at the present moment, they dare to say, nevertheless, that it will come to pass, sometime, somewhere.

What the Utopian literary form represents in human experience is essentially the quality of hope about the human situation and about the future. I belabor this point because it is critical. It is so easy to dismiss Utopias as the aberrations of distorted minds or as expressions of emotional instability. True, there are some weird pictures of the future that seem to spring full blown out of minds that have lost their bearing. But they are not characteristic either of the literature or of the concept of Utopia. Here we are face to face with the fundamental idea that through all generations men have gathered from the quality of life itself. No experience, no event at any particular moment in time exhausts the meaning and the "intent" of life as reflected in the way life lives itself out. This is why so very often men are unwilling to scale down the horizon of their hopes, dreams, and yearnings to the level of the events of their lives. So long as there is a conviction that a potential has not been actualized either in the individual, the society, or in the world, the rational necessity and possibility of a realized future must be honored. What the Utopia does is to give form and place to such actualization as a concrete existence, at least in the imagination and in the dream.

Now let us take a rather intimate look at certain large dreams of community in which men, voicing the needs and aspirations of their time, have given form and organization to the common life in accordance with particular plans and goals. Sometimes, as in the Book of Isaiah, idyllic fulfillment includes man and nature. Such a period is ushered in by an act of God, as in the creation of the world in Genesis; God is the be-all and end-all in it. We are given a vivid picture of the ideal and hope of kingship in Judah; the king has the *gift* of superhuman wisdom; he has this by direct endowment from God. It is this that the prophet means when he says:

> And the spirit of the Lord shall rest upon him
> The spirit of wisdom and understanding,
> The spirit of knowledge and the fear of the Lord.

> He shall not judge by what his eyes see
> Or decide by what his ears hear;
> But with righteousness he shall judge the poor,
> And decide with equity for the meek of the earth;
> And he shall smite the earth with the rod of his mouth
> And with the breath of his lips he shall slay the wicked.

Righteousness shall be the girdle of the waist,
And faithfulness the girdle of his loins,
And wolf shall dwell with lamb,
And the leopard shall lie down with the kid
And the calf and the lion and the fatling together
And a little child shall lead them.

The cow and the bear shall feed;
Their young shall lie down together;
And the lion shall eat straw like the ox,
The suckling child shall play over the hole of the asp.
And the weaned child shall put his hand on the adder's den.
They shall not hurt or destroy in all my holy mountain,
For the earth shall be full of the knowledge of the Lord
As the waters cover the sea.

Here the intent of the Creator in creation is that community shall be a literal fact in the fulfillment of life at every level. The actualization of this potential is the dream that is nourished in each expression of life. Animals and men alike share in this dream. Here we have an echo of the myths of creation when there was no initial enmity between man and animals. At a later point, certain experiences will be fully discussed in which man and animals established a living sense of community with each other.

I turn now to another kind of Utopia—Plato's *Republic*. This was a political Utopia dated roughly 427–347 B.C. These dates cover the general period during which Athens fought her long and disastrous war with Sparta. It was a time of defeat. In the *Republic* is to be found Plato's answer to the despair and disillusionment of his contemporary world. Plato rejects the idea that the contradictions of life are in themselves final. When society as he had known it was falling apart, it was a psychologically appropriate moment for the very foundations of social organization to be examined, and for the meaning and significance of justice to be considered in a community that was intentionally conceived and built. What he seeks to envision is an ideal community.

How does he propose to do it? It is interesting to observe that Plato is seeking to correct present evils by projecting a State in which these evils do not appear. Moral virtue is identical with political virtue in his State. The fundamental goal before him is the search for justice, since it seems easier to understand the meaning of justice when considering the State than when trying to separate the motives in the life of the solitary individual. The State has location, as it is a physical fact. It is a definite piece of land whose limits are determined by the necessities of the idea and where those who live within its boundaries are tied together by the ownership of common goods, common theaters, and so forth. There is a wide variety of common interests which can be satisfied by people who work, play, and think together. The State develops its function to meet the needs of its citizens. It is a city-region near enough land to supply the food needed by the inhabitants. But we need not tarry over the details of its topography. Each group of citizens lives in the section that has utility for its particular function or calling in the State.

There is a limited and controlled population, making it possible for the potential of each individual in the State to be actualized. The citizens live intentional lives—this is the true basis of their freedom. It is difficult for us to imagine what this is like because our own experience in community does not easily provide for intentional living. We are moved by wants and desires that are most often artifically created and stimulated. We order our lives in accordance with goals, the fulfillment of which leaves us world-weary, physically exhausted, and spiritually hungry. Plato does not want any group within his society to have reason to be happier than any other. He compares the community to a human being who is possessed of wisdom, valor, temperance, and justice. The first three virtues are related directly to a particular class in the community: wisdom to the rulers, valor to the defenders, and temperance to all classes. The latter by definition "is the ordering or controlling of certain pleasures or desires; this is curiously enough implied in the saying of 'a man being his own master.' "

There is also recognition of the dual potential in the soul of man, an insight shared by the creation accounts previously discussed. ". . . in the human soul there is a better and also a worse principle; and when the better has the worse under control, then a man is said to be master of himself; and this is a term of praise; but when owing to evil education, or association, the better principle, which is also the smaller, is overwhelmed by the greater mass of the worse—in this case he is blamed and is called the slave of self and unprincipled." The State, then, is called master of itself if in it the words temperance and self-mastery express the rule of the better part over the worse. If such is the case, then there is an essential harmony and integration within it.

The function of temperance both in the individual and in the State is to create and preserve harmony. Such harmony is possible only when the potentials of the State and its citizens are mutually realized. "Temperance . . . extends to the whole and runs through all the notes of the scale, and produces a harmony of the weaker and the stronger and the middle class, whether you suppose them to be stronger or weaker in wisdom or power or numbers or wealth, or anything else."

But what of justice in the State? For after all, this is the essential quest of the grand undertaking in the *Republic.* Justice has to do with private and public morality. A man may neither take what is another's, nor be deprived of what is his own. This takes us back to the original principle of the State: one man should practice one thing only, the thing to which his nature is best adapted. The question of who will determine this or how the individual will know for himself is given no satisfactory answer. Social justice, then, is defined as a condition in which every person has and does peacefully what it is his right to have and to do; he fills the place for which he is fitted. For the private, inner life of the individual, the same thing obtains. The faculties of the individual are as integrated in his inner life as the individual is integrated in the common life of the State. Here is the basis for a rigid, functional class structure. There is no psychological or moral problem for Plato here, because he reflects the age and the period in which he lived. Once it is assumed that men are born with the basic equipment that defines their place and function in society, then each is fulfilled when this potential is realized. From this point of view even the notion of justice is derived.

The fundamental error in this position is the assumption that a wisdom capable of determining the potential for the individual can ever be the unique and infallible knowledge of any person or group of persons, however wise and sensitive and intelligent they may be. The basic principle growing out of our working definition of community must not be forgotten. It is the experience in which the potential is being actualized. Always it is an open question as to the preciseness with which potential can be determined even by the individual himself. Certainly, it is intolerable to set up social categories or classes in the society, and then by such predetermination select individuals and their progeny who automatically keep carrying on to fill all vacancies in the rank and file.

Some attempt is made to meet the basic inequities of social stratification as far as the individual person is concerned. This is achieved through the work of the guardians or rulers. They have the power to administer what someone has aptly called "the medicinal lie." Every effort is made to keep the youth from any conditioning that would make them rebel against the society on behalf of their own fulfillment and self-realization. In short, the youth's sense of his own potential is given to him by the guardians and it becomes psychologically true and binding.

To summarize Plato's notion of Utopia, it is in order to quote the most famous of all the quotations from the *Republic*:

Until philosophers are kings, or the kings and princes of this world have the spirit and the power of philosophy, and political greatness and wisdom meet in one, and those commoner natures who pursue either to the exclusion of the other are compelled to stand aside, cities will never have rest from their evils,—no, nor the human race, as I believe,—and then only will this our State have a possibility of life and behold the light of day.

The meaning of the *Republic* for my purpose here lies in the fact that it reveals the possibility of communal living without the deprivations and the spiritual degeneration due to personal frustration and large collective conflicts. It makes the case that it is within the scope of the powers of mind and imagination to order a world in which the destiny of man is a good and healthful destiny. Despite the fact that the projection of the dream has all the basic elements of a fiction, the dream itself is a judgment upon life as Plato was living it, and it sprang out of the soil of that life. In this sense there is a reality to it that becomes a source of inspiration and reassurance to all those who were sharers in the common life of the period.

From at least the time of Plato to the present, Utopias have continued to move in and out on the horizon of men's minds. The literature is abundant and it reflects a certain persistence in the human spirit, running the entire gamut of human hopes, aspirations, and judgment. Some of the Utopias are fantastic in imagery, dealing with the bizarre, the esoteric, and the whole spectrum of the imagination. Some of them elect to pinpoint a particular aspect of disorder in contemporary society as the starting point and from there, in a vast projection of the imagination, a whole new order of correction and redemption is envisaged.

It is very clear that the religion of Christianity has had no small part in the dream of fulfillment for the children of men. The mood of other-worldliness has contributed to this development. The idea is that beyond the present order, with its frustrations, sin, and broken harmony, there is another order in which God will do without hindrance what human sin and frailty made it difficult to achieve in any grand scale in the present world. This would be achieved at the end of the age, when His Kingdom would be totally established, or at the end of life for the individual believer. Here we see, once again, the recognition that the contradictions of life are not final, that what men experience as private or collective disaster need not be regarded with helplessness by the Christian. To be sure the Christian is a pilgrim in the world. He is a member of the

"Colony of Heaven," to use the Pauline phrase. The Kingdom of God would be ushered in by Christ at a climactic moment in human history. The New Jerusalem would come down from the sky and all the anointed ones would be gathered up in its salvation. But the Book of Revelation speaks for itself:

Then I saw a great White Throne, and One who was seated thereon: from his presence earth and sky fled, no more to be found.
And I saw the dead, high and low standing before the throne, and books were opened—
Also another book, the book of Life, was opened—
And the dead were judged by what was written in these books, by what they had done . . .
   Then I saw the New Heaven and the new earth, for the first heaven and the first earth had passed away; and the sea is no more.
   And I saw the holy city, the new Jerusalem, descending from God out of heaven . . .
And I heard a loud voice out of the throne, crying,
Lo, God's dwelling place is with men,
With men will he dwell; they shall be his people,
And God will himself be with them:
He will wipe every tear from their eyes,
And death shall be no more—
No more wailing or crying or pain,
For the first things have passed away.

Continuing, the author gives substance and dimension to the New City:

So he carried me off, rapt in the Spirit, to a huge high mountain.
where he showed me the City, the holy Jerusalem, descending from God out of heaven, with the glory of God.
The sheen of it resembled some rare jewel like jasper, clear as crystal; it has a huge high wall with twelve gates . . . three gates on the east, three gates on the north, three gates on the south, and three gates on the west . . .
And the wall of the City has twelve foundation stones . . .
The foundation stones of the city wall are adorned with all sorts of precious stones,

And the City needs no sun or moon to shine upon it, for the Glory of God
illumines it, and the Lamp lights it up.
By its light will the nations walk
And into it will the kings of earth bring their glories . . .
Nothing profane, none who practices abomination or falsehood shall enter.
but those alone whose names are written in the Lamb's Book of Life.

In essence, here are all the elements of Utopia, with the important difference that it is not made by the hands of man. It is a
specific creation by God, as seen by the Seer of Patmos, in the same
way that, in the creation account, the world and all therein was
made. It is a postponement into a future life of all the real good that
was denied in the present life. It is not open to all. There operates
here a profound principle of selection—all doctrines of salvation
seem to be involved with some form of character discrimination.
For those who are saved the full realization of all their radiant
possibilities are available to them. Whatever the present experiences may be, for those who feel that they are saved, the transcendent future holds a fulfillment not possible in the present. The
intent of the Creator is blocked, frustrated in time, but He is the
Creator of time; hence His intent will become manifest, if not in
time, then out of time. As Job says, "With or without my flesh, I
will see God."

The problem raised for those who are not of the Faith is not
resolved. There is something exclusive about all Utopias and this
is ever their tragic flaw. But they do reveal what the dreamer thinks
of as the highest end, the most authentic unfolding of life at its best
and highest. And this is important for our basic concept, despite its
other-worldly aspects.

It remains now to take a summary look at a more precisely
worldly Utopia than has been considered thus far in our discussion. Near the end of the Middle Ages, Sir Thomas More, Chan-
cellor under Henry VIII, wrote *Utopia*. His name has become
synonymous with the word itself. In *Utopia* we see a setting in
which the chief end in community is to have men grow to the
fullest stature of their species. Such can be accomplished only in a

community in which each member is able to share fully.

The Portuguese scholar Raphael Hythloday tells the story of this fabulous commonwealth. He is shown to be a man disenchanted with the life of his times. The contradictions and paradoxes abound on every side. Much of what he describes has an all-too-familiar ring: many of the rich thrive on the poor, the small farmer is forced from the land by the large combines, soldiers home from the wars find no jobs and slight welcome, luxury and misery stand in defiant contrast to each other. The poor beseech and the proud filch, vagrants and thieves are jailed, executed. The whole world is gray with misery.

Hythloday's solemn commentary is: "As long as there is any property and while money is the standard of all other things, I cannot think that a nation can be governed justly or happily; not just because the best things will fall to the worse men; not happily because all things will be divided among a few, the rest being left to be absolutely miserable."

The opening up of the New World and the renascence of French philosophy made possible the kindling of a new dream concerning the human situation and its possibility. A new Utopia fires the imagination and reveals their hopes about the personal and collective destiny of the individual and the race.

Utopia is a place. It existed in More's imagination. "The Isle of Utopia contains in breadth 200 miles, saving that it comes in towards both ends . . . which fashion the whole island like the new moon. Between the two corners the sea runs in dividing them by eleven miles. . . .

"There are in the island 54 cities . . . all set and situated alike, and in all points fashioned alike, none of them distant from the next above one day's journey afoot." The unit of political life is the city region, as in the *Republic.*

The economic base of the society is agriculture. There is diversified farming—eggs are hatched by incubators. Everybody knows the science and art of agriculture. There are special trades and crafts. There is no menial work, as such. The chief rulers are called magistrates; their main responsibility is to see that no one lives in idleness.

There is also a planned economy, covering both production and distribution of goods. Every care is given to see that the population of each city is stabilized. When the number grows too large in any given city, its excess is put into other families where the population is below the established average. "If the multitude throughout the whole island exceed the due number, they choose out of every city certain citizens and build up a town under their own laws in the neighboring land, where the inhabitants have much unoccupied ground. If the inhabitants will not dwell with them, to be ordered by their laws, they drive them out of their bounds; and if they resist they make war against them."

Everyone is sure that he shall always be supplied so he does not have to hoard. There is no fear of want, which, according to More, makes men greedy and lustful. There is a sharp distinction between true and false pleasures. All pleasure is false that has some sting or bitterness in it, such as love for fine clothes, or heaping of wealth, or gambling, and so forth. The true pleasures are those which have to do with the body and the mind.

To the soul they give intelligence and that delectation that comes from contemplation of truth or the good life past. The pleasures of the body occur when delight is felt by the senses as when we eat and drink, or when itching is eased with scratching, or in the quiet or upright state of the body; for every man's proper health is delectable of itself and is the foundation of all pleasure. . . .

They count the pleasures of the mind the chiefest of all. The chief part of them come from the exercise of virtue and consciousness of the good life. . . . They begin every dinner and supper by reading something that pertains to good manners and virtue.

On the Island of Utopia people have a chance to develop their own positive and constructive potentialities. The assumption is that this can best and perhaps only be done in the kind of controlled environment dedicated to this end. The individual experiences cannot be separated from the collective and communal experience; they are linked together inseparably. Here we see a complete rejection of the way of life that was the climate in which More lived but not as an end in itself. There is another alternative, another possibility. The essence of it is already in the mind and spirit of man. The Island of Utopia is its, *for instance.*

Mumford, in his story of Utopia, has a most creative summary of the total meaning of Utopias in the life of man:

> To cultivate the soil rather than simply to get away with a job; to take food and drink rather than to earn money; to think and dream and invent, rather than to increase one's reputation; in short, to grasp the living reality and spurn the shadow. This is the substance of the utopian way of life. In this utopia of the new world, every man has the opportunity to be a man because no one has the opportunity to be a monster.

Community as the Utopian dream is a part of the basic aspiration of the human spirit. It is not important at any particular time and place that the Utopia does not become literal fact; it reveals, however, what the imagination of man has to say about the true possibility of the human spirit. This dream expresses what man sees as his potential if he were at liberty to fashion a world in accordance with his needs, his hopes, his destiny. Deep within himself he knows that if he settles for anything less than this, he denies the profound intent of his own spirit, which is one with the intent of the Creator.

We turn now to an examination of some of the ways by which community is realized in the self-conscious relationship between man and other conscious expressions of life in his environment.

V

The Search in the Common Consciousness

Ask the very beasts, and they will teach you;
Ask the wild birds—they will tell you;
Crawling creatures will instruct you,
Fish in the sea will inform you;
For which of them knows not that this
    is the Eternal's way,
In whose control lives every living soul,
And the life of man—Job.

In a lecture some forty years ago by Dr. William W. Keen, professor emeritus of surgery at Jefferson Medical College in Philadelphia, there is a description of surgery performed on the brain of a young woman suffering from epilepsy. She had observed that the attack usually started in her left thumb and then spread to the rest of her body. The surgeon reasoned that if he could prevent the attack from starting in the thumb, the entire fit would not come to pass. Initially, the problem was to locate the precise center in the brain that controlled the motor action in the thumb. Drawing upon his knowledge derived from animal experimentation, he knew where the precise center was located. When the doctor opened the skull of the patient and identified the spot corresponding to the thumb center in animals (i.e., the great toe of the front foot), he cut out a small cube from each side. "The human brain center and the animal center for the thumb were proved to be precisely identical."

Observations and the experimentations abound that indicate not merely a common origin for man and nonhuman animals, for the wide variety of living forms on the earth, but that in the growth and development of forms of life much of the journey is identical. Life seeking to realize itself in any given expression draws upon a wide range of experience and uses identical devices, gadgets, and utilitarian forms. Thus, living things do not merely have in common their origin and the fact that each is conscious, but they also seem to have levels of communication that tend to make for a harmonious relationship. The creation accounts seem to take this fact for granted; it is the logic of the process that brought forms of life into being in the first place. What men have discovered through the ages is that not only is there an affinity that the mind has for the external world, but also that there is an affinity between man's own consciousness and the many forms of consciousness around him. The more aware man becomes of this the more he discovers that his own sense of self seems to be greatly enlarged, and all of life seems to be more intimately a part of him and he a part of it.

It is important to observe that this awareness may be experienced by two different forms of life without a previous history of association. What I am suggesting is that there is such a thing as a general experience of life that two forms may share at the same moment in time without resistance and without threat.

The following experience illustrates my meaning: When I was a small boy I went across the meadow to visit with one of my chums. I was running around the house when I heard a voice, which came from a knock on the windowpane. I looked up to see my friend's father standing in the room. As soon as he caught my attention he motioned for me to turn around and come into the house through the front door. When I entered the room he pointed through an open window. There I saw his baby girl, less than a year old, sitting in the sand playing with a rattlesnake. It was an amazing and deeply frightening experience to watch. The child would turn the snake over on its side and do various things with him; the snake would crawl around her, then crawl back. It was apparent that they were playing together.

I was sent back into the yard to stand guard to keep anyone from coming around the house to frighten them. For if their harmony were broken by sudden disharmony created by noise or sudden movement, there would have been violence on earth. After a while the baby grew tired of playing, turned away, and started crawling toward the back steps; the snake crawled towards the woods on the edge of the yard. It was then that the father drew a bead on the snake's head with his shotgun, killing him instantly. It was as if two different expressions of life, normally antagonistic to each, had dropped back into some common ground and there reestablished a sense of harmony through which they were relating to each other at a conscious level.

More obvious kinds of communication take place between members of the same species or family. The life that is realizing itself in each one cannot be regarded as a distinct undertaking, but rather it must be seen as a single expression or activity, or seen as an organism. The basic aim is always the same: to aid the process by which potentials are actualized. For it is only in this way that the continuity of the species can be guaranteed. And for the particular species and the individuals in it, this is community. The point of each solitary form of life is that in it life itself may not be defeated.

First, then, individual harmony must obtain within the particular organism, then within the group of organisms that are immediately organically related to one another. On behalf of this kind of endeavor a wide variety of methods of communication is employed. Since the individual and collective harmonies are dependent upon nourishment and reproduction, these two aspects of life are always guaranteed as far as possible by the behavior pattern or the reflex action of the individuals. The basic purpose of all communication finds its meaning here. The mating calls, the particular sounds indicating danger or fear—these are all commonplace. The individual howler among the Central American howling monkeys communicates his message, giving forth his reaction to at least nine different situations; one sound indicates an invasion, another indicates merely that the group is being threatened or that the individual howler is suspicious, or one monkey suggests a change in direction that he wants the group to take.

Robert Ardrey comments that the crow distinguishes the hunter from other men not by the gun he carries but by the dead bird in his hand. It seems that the personal identification becomes rooted in the consciousness of every member of the flock by the timbre of the outcry.

Other flocks, which have not themselves witnessed the murder of their kind, will hear and take up the cry; and so the hunter's bad reputation may be spread through a whole region. He may change his hunting ways. . . . Even so, generations of crows yet unborn will learn that this particular man has a crow record, and must be regarded for all times as a bad risk to crow welfare. So animal society becomes the permanent repository for animal experience, surviving the death of individual members.

Of course, we do not know precisely how to assess the wide variety of means by which insects and animals establish overt communication with one another. But where there are sounds that can be heard by the human ear, particular sounds and the reactions to them are observed over a long enough period to provide the basis for some judgment as to their meaning. Suffice it to say that some kind of code is operative on behalf of the "intent" of life as we see it functioning under our scrutiny.

The whole process becomes more complicated when communication between man and other forms of life is under examination. It is not unreasonable to me that some elemental communication can take place between man and flowers or plants. What I am about to say may seem to be a trick of the imagination, but several years ago when my roses were not doing well, each night I would go out and express orally my concern for their well-being, even to the point of gently patting the branches, not merely because of the thorns. It may be that what I recognized as a response in terms of growth and blossom may have been due to the extra attention that I gave them because of my concern.

When we turn to communication with animals the ground seems more secure. The organic basis for responsive behavior may be found in the observation made by Dr. Keen at the beginning of this chapter. At any rate, the whole area is worth exploration because the basis of community as a self-conscious and deliberate expression in the society of men may be rooted here.

When I was ten, I was a delivery boy for a meat market in our town. I had delivered an order to the kitchen of a particular family and was in the act of mounting my bicycle when a large Dalmatian dog, without making a sound, jumped from a nearby porch, ran between my right leg and the bicycle and tore a large piece of flesh out of my leg muscle. I had not noticed him before the attack. The fright and the pain gave a fundamental shock to my nervous system. So profound was the trauma that even to this day I must make a disciplined effort to be at ease in the presence of any dog, however friendly he may be. It is a battle that must always be won in initial contact, or my muted panic takes over. Because of my love for dogs, each encounter has its own unique challenge until a basis of community is established and maintained.

One illustration will suffice. I was invited to spend the afternoon visiting a family in a town where I was a visiting lecturer for several months. The first time I went there I was accompanied by a member of the family. We came through the kitchen and were greeted by the stirring bark of a large German shepherd dog. As we entered the son held the dog by the collar while his mother spoke to the dog. He continued to bark, his eyes set on me in a manner that was completely unnerving. I knew once again that my work was cut out for me whether or not I ever intended to return to the farm for other visits. I made my decision and above his barks I spoke to the dog, calling him by name, announcing that we would have to learn to know each other. He followed us into the living room where we sat on a couch. He stood in the door until we were all settled, never taking his eyes from me. At length, he lay down in the doorway with his face in my direction. After a few minutes of general conversation I was left alone in the living room. Now he raised his head looking directly at me. When I was completely in charge of myself I said, "I know your job is to keep watch, so today I do not blame you. You are just doing your job. But I want to know you and I am sure that you will like me when you know me." He simply looked at me without making a sound or moving any part of his body. I was relieved that there was no obvious sign of anger or fear.

When one of the members of the family returned, I asked her to sit near me on the couch to explain some pictures. Immediately the dog came over and rested his head on her hand, always looking at me. Then she explained to him that I was a friend.

Again I was left alone. This time he did not go to his post at the door but lay down nearby. A period of some five minutes had passed when I turned completely in his direction, calling him by name, saying, "Do you know why I react to you as I do? Well, I'll tell you. When I was a small boy . . . and so forth. Now despite that experience I like dogs very much. Do you know something? You have the largest paws I have ever seen on a dog. Since I have been a man I have had two dogs. Do you know what their names were? Barriemore and Kropotkin." By this time he had gotten up from the floor, stood on his feet in a lazy manner, and started walking toward the door. He looked back at me, then stopped as if he were listening.

Meanwhile, I continued my conversation. "It's too bad that you don't want to stay. If you will stay with me so that we can really get acquainted, I'll scratch you where you itch but can't scratch. And that is a wonderful feeling! Come on over, I'll be careful to begin in the obvious place, like under your collar." I looked steadily at him and waited. Slowly he turned and walked in my direction, paused, and then came over to me. Despite everything, I could hardly manage my inner tension. He sniffed, beginning down at my ankles, then my trousers, and finally he rested his huge head in the crevice between my knees. For the first time now I touched him, running my hand along the back of his neck, and gently I began a scratching-massaging motion until my fingers were under the chain around his neck. Now the real work of scratching began.

All the while I was talking, telling him about my two dogs but watching his eyes and being aware of his reflexes or responses. At one point I noticed that his eyes began to get that far-away look and his eyelids closed ever so slightly. With that as a clue my hands moved to his long nose, which I scratched with delicate skill, all the way to beneath the eyelids and above. His eyes were half closed now. "Are you ready now for the real goody or have you had enough for now? I am in no hurry, it is up to you." I stopped, waited but did not remove my hand. He swished his big bushy tail, nuzzled his head more deeply between my knees, and waited, looking at me. I took this to mean: keep going. So I did. With the palm of my hand I made a rotating motion, with increasing pressure on the outside of his right ear. His delight in this was obvious. With great care I took my index finger and massaged the inside of his outer ear. I covered all the inner surface with my probing finger, massaging and pressing, pressing and massaging, until his eyes closed entirely. When I finished, he sniffed me over from shoes to knees, turned and walked out of the room.

In the weeks that followed, each time I came he stood guard with his frightening bark but it lasted a shorter time on each succeeding visit. Finally when he heard my voice he would stop barking. When I entered the house he would come over to greet me. As always, I had my moments, but from the first day's adventure our understanding deepened. The last time I saw him we played together for a few minutes in the yard and had our picture taken.

I am convinced that there is a ground of unity between animals and man of which any oral communication is but symbolic or vehicular. The oral communication must be of such sounds that they unlock the door between. How this is done we do not know.

The notion that man is the higher animal and all others are lower, the development of elaborate self-consciousness in man, the ability to think reflectively that is a use of the mind that gives it the sense of living its own life apart from the body—all of these and kindred ideas have erected a great wall between man and other animals. The sense of separateness from the rest of nature is so marked that man tends to see himself as being over against nature. In defense of this conceit, various dogmas and even theologies have been developed. My point is not that the sense of separateness is not authentic but merely that it is not absolute. Life is always seeking to realize itself in myriad forms and patterns of manifestation. These forms and manifestations include the organic structure as well as diffused consciousness or awareness at its most elemental level and self-consciousness in its profoundest expression.

Fear keeps the doors between sealed. It is a basic response to threat. Over so many years men and animals have lived essentially apart from each other and the predatory instinct, particularly among men, has been so crucial in their survival that any notion of community that moves out beyond the protective enclosure is fatuous and illusory. But where there is deliberate acceptance between men and animals, a fresh possibility of enlarged meaning for each emerges. I suspect that under such circumstances even the potential of each life undergoes a radical expansion. Once the acceptance has taken place, even ancient enmity begins to give way and new meanings emerge.

In Hotchner's *Papa Hemingway* there is an arresting illustration of the possibilities of communication once acceptance is assured. According to his story, Hemingway enjoyed going to the Ringling Brothers circus when it came to New York, and he had a lifetime pass given to him by his friend John Ringling North. On this occasion, accompanied by Hotchner, Hemingway went to Madison Square Garden some time before the circus opened. They found their way below where the animals were in their cages. It should be pointed out that Hemingway thought that circus animals were more intelligent than other animals because in their experience of acceptance by their trainers there had been a greater development on their part. The acceptance enlarged the potential, or so it seemed.

When they went down below Hemingway was drawn to the gorilla. Naturally, the keeper was quite nervous about having any man, and particularly a stranger to the circus, get too close to his charge. But Hemingway

stood close to the cage and talked to the gorilla in a staccato cadence and kept talking, and finally the gorilla, who appeared to be listening, was so moved he picked up his plate of carrots and dumped it on top of his head; then he started to whimper; sure signs, the keeper said, of his affection.

Naturally this created quite a sensation among all the keepers and trainers. All of them wanted him to see how well their particular charges could respond. But he insisted that the only wild animal with whom he had real talking rapport was the bear. When he stopped in front of the polar bear cage, this animal was swinging back and forth across the enclosure.

"He is very nasty, Mr. Hemingway," the bear keeper said. "I think you're better off talking to this brown bear, who has a good sense of humor."

"I should get through to him," Ernest said, staying with the polar bear, "but I haven't talked bear talk for some time and I may be rusty." The keeper smiled. Ernest edged in close to the bars. He began to speak to the bear in a soft, musical voice totally unlike the gorilla language, and the bear stopped pacing. Ernest kept on talking, and the words, or I should say sounds, were unlike any I had ever heard. The bear backed up a little and grunted, and then it sat on its haunches and, looking straight at Ernest, it began to make a series of noises through its nose, which made it sound like an elderly gentleman with severe catarrh.

The keeper was completely astounded and expressed it with a vibrant oath. As Hemingway walked away from the cage the bear stared after him, bewildered.

" 'It's Indian talk,' Ernest said. 'I'm part Indian. Bears like me. Always have.' "

To many people even communication between animals of the same kind is unthinkable. But any serious thought concerning or observation of various animals and insects will reveal what may be called the language of the kind. Within the particular family or class grouping, through millions of years, there have developed behavior patterns found useful in the unfolding potential of each. The squeak of baby bats in a dark grotto may sound like bedlam to the human ear but to the individual mother her baby's squeak is different from all the rest. And this is not surprising. There is a private life of every living thing—a living from the inside. This is where the "intent" of creation is dramatically in evidence, when the potential gathers for the push into realization.

I wonder what it feels like to try to get inside? In one of my most beloved books, referred to earlier, Jane Steger's *Leaves From a Secret Journal,* she muses on this idea.

What in the world makes these green leaves? Oh no, I don't want to know what they are composed of. A botanist might tell me that. What I want to know is why the sap ever started to run up the tree, up the trunk, along the limbs, into the buds, to spread them out into leaves. Perhaps the way to find out would be to get inside the tree one's self, a nebulous personality, to run with the sap up the trunk, out the limbs, into the leaves and maple keys, and there hear the command to stop. The end is as amazing as the beginning. Why does the urge of life cease with leaves and seed vessels? How does it know when to stop—when its type is completed? If this command to halt didn't come out the right moment, the breath of life that is in the tree might go on beyond leaves and bloom into all sorts of green fantastic abortions that would spoil the type. . . . It *is* a miracle that trees stop with themselves—that maple trees are only maple trees, apple trees only apple trees, and oak trees only oaks. The urge of life might so easily have flowed on into a maelstrom of confusion, a sort of crazy quilt of creation.

The same, of course, is true of every type. Why do pigs stop at pigs, and human beings at human beings. . . . Each type may have come up from something else, and be slowly drifting on to another development; nevertheless, at each stage it is itself, and not a confused medley. . . . The urge of life always amazed me, but I never until now realized the marvel of its stopping when each creation is completed. . . .

I would like to get inside of my maple and see what it feels like to be a tree. Perhaps I was a tree once long ago, at one stage of my journey from an atom to an angel. . . . I can scarcely remember the time when I did not have this inexplicable yearning to get inside of growing things and taste, as it were, their consciousness.

Leonard Dubkin refers to the same idea in relating his experience with bats. By accident he discovered a colony of bats in an empty Chicago lot. Through many days and nights he learned the habits of the colony and witnessed the actual birth of an albino whom he called the White Lady. This became the title of his story. The little albino bat and he became friends; she was able to accustom herself to the scent of his fingers so that he would be recognized and ultimately trusted. On the point under discussion here Dubkin says:

Science can tell us many things about the other creatures around us, our neighbors on the planet earth; it can give us a detailed explanation of the physical make-up of each species, of how it lives and gets its food and raises its young. But science cannot tell us what it is like to be a bat or an elephant or a fly, it cannot probe into the inner consciousness of a living being and peer into the secret reactions to its existence. And while it is important that science should discover and announce the facts about other living beings on the earth, it seems to me equally important that a man should occasionally step away from his constant association with other human beings, and immerse himself in lives different from his own, steep himself so far as possible in the personality and subjective perceptiveness of other creatures. So that even though I had not, alas, discovered any new theory about bats, even though I had not been the one to prove that bats find their way in the dark by the use of high frequency sounds, there was some consolation in the knowledge that I was closer to the bats in the grotto, more intimate with them and more appreciative of their style of life, than any scientist intent on his experiments could ever be.

It is entirely possible that when a man seems to be communicating with an animal, he is merely projecting onto the animal his own frame of reference and thereby making a false estimate or assessment of what is transpiring. It may be that it is a trick of the mind causing him to read into the behavior of the animal the response that another human being would make. Obviously we are moving in a realm in which it is very difficult to separate fact from fancy. This is not to say that fancy does not have its own reality.

If, however, we begin with the concept of the fundamental unity of life that seems to be the logic of all that investigation, exploration, and imagination reveal about beginnings, then it does not seem unreasonable to make the assumption that the context that defines or limits any particular expression of life is but a variation of the one basic theme. We do not know what life is because we have no tools for isolating it. But what we do know is that life is characterized by activity in some form, that directiveness and creativeness are inherent in life. If one form of life can transcend or get beyond the wall, barrier, or context that separates it from another form of life, then essential unity of life is confirmed to that extent. Out of each such experience one gets an insight that can be applied to myriad experiences with many forms of life. The tough thing is that the inherited notion that the different expressions of life are not only unique but are absolutely and completely different makes the idea of an underlying unity meaningless. Very readily one would agree that there ought to be or must be some adequate ground for establishing the basis for unity within a given group or classification, say of animals, or insects, or man. But to hazard the possibility that the same applies *across* such a classification is to indulge in a fiction.

It is worth noting that from time immemorial men have felt that there was a universal language prior to the creation of symbols of communication such as words. This language included all living things as well as man. We see this idea in its most beautiful and poetic expression in the creation myths. I am here thinking of something more fundamental than any of the illustrations previously given here.

There seems to be a difference between confirming the unity of life among one's own kind and confirming the unity of life across kingdoms or species. In the latter instance the mind temporarily gives up its sense of individuality and drops back into an original creative continuum in which boundaries of the human self are temporarily transcended. The awareness of conscious meaning is not lost; it is merely enlarged.

An Italian duke who was a doctor and administrator of Italy's former African colonies wrote out of his experiences a book entitled *A Grave for a Dolphin*. There are many interesting stories in it about children, animals, and magic. The story of interest for my purpose is called "A Sermon for Wart Hogs." It is the account of the Prior of Barentu's ability to talk meaningfully to animals. For the Big Father (as he was called), chatting with animals was a matter of course and he had no doubt at all that the animals understood what he meant. He was not merely communicating or establishing a kind of vague response reaction. He was sure that he shared ideas with animals and that they in turn understood him. It is not clear from the account whether the process worked in reverse. It was said that he looked at the world of animals from an angle of his own. He did not believe that man was the hub of the universe, but that man was one of the billions of beings to "whom God had granted the gift of life."

The account relates that when the crops came up and began to grow, the custom was to drive a series of poles into the ground and upon them build crows' nests in which boys would seclude themselves armed with slings, in order to keep the wart hogs from coming in to destroy the crops. It was observed that the Big Father took no such defensive measures for his crop. When he was asked about it he said that the wart hogs would not dare lay waste land belonging to the Mission. He was convinced that they were sensible animals and would always listen to reason. It had been made very clear to them that the Mission's harvest fed scores and scores of people who had no land of their own.

All of this came out in conversation between the author and the Prior when the former was an overnight guest of the Mission. The precise statement of the Big Father was:

> I speak to the wart hogs every year. Every year at the end of the heavy rains, when the maize-cobs begin to swell, I tell them how many families

get a living from our crops and beg them not to desolate our fields; till now, I must say, they have always complied with my desire. This year also, when the moon is full, I shall speak again to the poor brutes; I should be glad if you would come with me.

Later that evening when all the monks had gone to sleep the Big Father and his guest walked quietly out into the yard where the full moon was in complete play. Together they walked for a mile or two until they came to a glade where they sat on the roots of a large tree. Here the Big Father with bowed head began praying; in the surrounding silence the snap of the beads under his fingers was clearly audible. When the prayer was over the Prior became very alert.

Carrying his head slightly over his left shoulder, his eyes riveted on the trees across the glade, quivering with suppressed excitement, he strained his ears, letting the beads dangle idly from his hands.

Far away a stifled throbbing echoed through the forest and the big trunks gave it back; scattered among the trees stocky shapes were looming in the darkness, stumbling over the roots, grunting and grubbing in the high grass not daring to come in the open.

The Big Father stood up and dragging his feet, stumbled to the center of the glade: with bent head and clasped hands he was praying. In front of him here and there like gargoyles between the spires of a cathedral, fanged snouts peeped amid the trunks, and when the throng of fourfooted monsters grew thicker, some of the bolder pushed forward, furrowing rushes and reeds.

At my left the massive bulk of an old wart hog tottered out into the glade; its skin was hairless, wrinkled and creased, the mane had shrunk to a few faded tufts and in the lumpish knotty muzzle the eyes were glassy and lifeless. The old patriarch, worn out with age and infirmities, was blind; two young hogs flanked it and with its snout the blind ancestor clung hold of the tail of a female who acted as guide.

The Prior spoke to the assembly of wart hogs. He spoke in the indigenous language of the area. It was a sharing of himself with other expressions of life, but from the inside of life rather than the outside. At the end of his short speech he said a brief prayer, after which he raised his hands and blessed the wart hogs, who were not more than three yards distant from him. When this was over and not until, they moved back into the forest in the midst of many snorts and grunts. When the Prior and the Duke returned to the Mission's square, they went immediately into the church. While the Mass was being said the Duke tried to sort out the confusing conflicting, and amazing set of ideas and impressions in his mind. It was not as if he did not know something firsthand about wart hogs. As a doctor, on many occasions he had patched up Africans whose sides had been ripped up by one of these animals. He had seen dogs completely annihilated by their fangs. And yet he had seen these same animals behave as if they were a quiet flock of lambs around the Big Father. They seemed to listen to his speech as if they understood it. And who was there to gainsay it?

These were some of the thoughts that he tried to sort out in his mind:

What unknown power had dragged the blind hog out of the forest? Who had told the young sow to lead it into the glade? Why had the hogs slipped away after the Prior's benediction? Obviously, with that gesture he had dismissed them; but then, how had he managed to summon the herd? Did he really know how to extract the strictest obedience from wild animals?

One is reminded of the Little Flowers of Saint Francis, when he said to the wild wolf of Gubbio:

Then said Saint Francis, "Friar Wolf, since it pleaseth thee to make and observe this peace, I promise to obtain for thee, so long as thou livest, a continual sustenance from the men of this city, so that thou shalt no more suffer hunger, for well I ween that thou hast wrought all this evil to satisfy thy hunger. But after I have won this favour for thee, Friar Wolf, I desire that thou promiseth me to do hurt neither to man nor beast. Dost thou promiseth me this?" And the wolf bowed his head and gave clear token that he promised these things.

Before discussing these accounts in terms of community, it is in order to examine a different variation on the same basic theme of communication with animals. In 1953, I read the galleys of a book written by Allen Boone called *Kinship With All Life*. In no sense does Boone make any pretension to be scientific—what he undertakes is very clear in the foreword. It is his insight that man has broken an original harmony between himself and all living things. He believes that this lost harmony can be restored if men learn to move in genuine good fellowship with their own species and all other creatures. "In support of this faith, I have set down in the following pages the true stories of a number of unconventional relationships with animals, reptiles, insects, and even bacteria. None of these ventures was planned or expected. They came into experience as part of the gracious unfoldment of life itself." His position is that when a man becomes properly humble and open to the instruction of his fellow creatures, they share with him their cumulative wisdom. It was his experience that perfect understanding and cooperation between human and all other forms of life is unfailing whenever human beings are free to enter into the relationship.

Boone's great teacher was the famous movie star, Strongheart, a German Shepherd who came from a long line of champions noted for their ability to qualify as work, police, and war dogs. Strongheart was bred in Germany and was brought to this country to be trained as a performer before the motion picture camera. His fame was instant; soon he was among the most famous of all movie personalities.

As a special favor to his trainer and manager, Boone agreed to keep Strongheart as his guest for a number of weeks. They were properly introduced and comfortably established as friends in the new and temporary home. Very careful instructions had been given concerning the care and attention that the famous dog required. Always Strongheart was talked to as though he were an intelligent human being.

When they arrived in their new home for the first time, Strongheart jumped out of the car as soon as the door was opened, ran up the steps, opened the front door with his teeth, and proceeded to go from room to room in the house, checking all the closets, and so on. When he had completed his survey he returned to his host, gave the back of his hand a slight dab with his tongue, and continued out into the yard to complete his investigation.

The problem Boone faced was twofold: He had to accept the fact that Strongheart was a most unusual animal, to say the least, with what appeared to be well-integrated mental equipment that had to be explored sensitively if it were to be understood. In the second place, he had to try to grasp what were the lines of kinship between them—"individual expressions of a highly intelligent universe." From the beginning there seemed to be evidence of an extra "something" at work in the dog to which the most revolutionary adjustment had to be made. For instance, one beautiful spring morning after many days of rain, Boone was seated at his typewriter doing his stint of creative work for the day. "Shall I be a man and finish this writing job, or shall I be a mouse, quit the whole thing and take Strongheart into the hills for the rest of the day and evening?" he asked himself. The decision to be a mouse carried the day.

Scarcely a few seconds had passed before the dog came bursting into the house in a tizzy. He landed near the chair in which Boone was seated, gave his hand a dab with the tongue, then rushed into the bedroom to get an old sweater that was a part of the hiking equipment. Back into the bedroom he went to get the old blue jeans. Another trip brought, one after the other, the walking boots. When these were assembled the dog brought Boone's Irish walking stick. Now he proceeded to bark and jump around with real excitement until at last Boone was dressed, ready for the hike.

What had happened here? How did the dog know what was going on in the mind of this man? Is there some explanation that can account for all the facts or must we settle for the description of what happened and leave it there? In a conversation with a man called Mojave Dan in his home in the desert, Boone tried to find some answers to his questions. The only comment he was able to elicit, bearing upon his problem of understanding his relationship with Strongheart, were these words: "There's facts about dogs and there's opinions about them. The dogs have the facts, and the humans have the opinions. If you want facts about a dog, always get them straight from the dog. If you want opinions, get them from the human."

One of the changes growing out of Dan's advice was regular conversation and reading sessions with Strongheart. I may add that among the long list of written instructions left by the dog's trainer was the requirement to read a little poetry to him each day. It was during these sessions that Boone declares that he changed his attitude toward the dog. He stopped treating him as a dog and began dealing with him as an equal *and* a companion. Thus the "kinship barriers came tumbling down." Slowly the teaching roles were reversed. Strongheart became the teacher and Boone the pupil. "My teacher and trainer needed only himself, a bit of encouragement from me, my undivided attention, and enough space in which to operate. My study period was practically continuous; as long as Strongheart was observable, school was in session and I was being taught."

There was one experience that impressed me beyond all the others. Strongheart led Boone up a very ragged climb when they were making one of their jaunts away from the familiar route. They came to the top of a high hill in the late afternoon. In the distance was the Pacific Ocean, which lay like an enormous pane of glass. The whole panorama was a glorious sheen of crimson reflected by the sinking sun. Together they stood watching the sunset. At length Strongheart walked to a nearby ledge, sat down, and resumed watching. Boone joined him, sitting in a position that enabled him to watch the sunset and the dog. It was evident that the dog was taking in the whole impact of the setting; a strange and almost eerie quiet settled over his entire body while his eyes took on a "distant view." But when Boone shifted his position so as to follow the direction of the dog's gaze, he discovered that the dog was looking at a point above the horizon line. "He was staring off into fathomless space. Out there beyond the ability of my human senses to identify what it was, something was holding the big dog's attention like a magnet! And it was giving him great satisfaction, great contentment, great peace of mind."

This experience is very like one in a book called *The Dynasty of Abu,* by Ivan Anderson. He comments that not only elephants but several other kinds of animals have been seen to stand silently every morning and evening, usually just about at dawn and sunset, whether the sun itself be visible or not. He continues: "This has been reported by all manner of people through the ages; and if it is true who is willing to say that the animals are not then indulging in some emotion that we might justly call 'praying,' even if they be but moments of wide-awake silence, complete relaxation or apparent blankness."

There is an unmistakably clear description of certain monkeys in West Africa whose custom it was to sit in the top of the jungle trees quietly facing the rising or setting sun. The author describes the feeling of awe that this inspired in him as he watched them. He was drawn to them in a strange and uncanny way. Soon he found himself "praying" with them. In order to be open to such experiences he had to break down his misconstructed intellectual armor and accept as valid the suggestion that the animals at such times were actually "praying."

In *Kinship With All Life,* the point that Boone is making, not only in the story of his experience with Strongheart, but also in the accounts dealing with ants, rattlesnakes, skunks, and houseflies, is always the same. It is possible for the individual to move out beyond the particular context by which his life is defined and relate to other forms of life from inside their context. This means that there is a boundless realm of which all particular life is but a manifestation. This center is the living thing in man or animal. If a man or an animal can function out of that center, then the boundaries that limit and define can be transcended.

I am not unmindful of the reaction to these pages that would indicate a misguided and overdeveloped sentimentality characteristic of certain animal lovers. It well may be that there is no basis in fact for authentic intelligible communication between man and other animals. But the fact remains that where such experiences are recorded or reported, there is at work an important kind of communication. The interpretation may be erroneous, but the sense of being in touch across the barriers that divide is itself an important part of the reality of the experience. If the mind of man has an affinity with the world external to him, and if in his origin and continuity he is a child of nature, then the experience of being consciously in touch with other forms of conscious life around him is a vital part of all life that seeks ever to realize itself in its many forms. When men ignore this, then their behavior very easily becomes wantonly destructive, and in their blindness, ignorance, or arrogance they force expressions of life around them to fall short of actualizing their potential. In the extent to which this takes place, community itself is defeated in the life all around us. If this is done, it may be that man himself is cut off from actualizing his potential and thus cannot know community in himself and in the world of his fellow.

It is now time to apply my thesis to the private and collective life of man.

> Truth is within ourselves; it takes no rise
> From outward things, what'er you may believe.
> There is an utmost center in us all,
> Where truth abides in fulness; and around,
> Wall upon wall, the gross flesh hems it in,
> This perfect, clear perception—which is truth.
> A baffling and perverting carnal mesh
> Binds it, and makes error; and to know
> Rather consists in opening out a way
> Whence the imprisoned splendour may escape,
> Than in effecting entry for a light
> Supposed to be without.

> —ROBERT BROWNING, "PARACELSUS"

VI

The Search in Identity

I have already undertaken in broad outline to indicate the path along which my investigation, stimulated by deep passion, has taken me in my effort to explore the grounds for community in the arena that marks the drama of man's life on the planet. It may be an open question as to the extent to which "goal-seeking" in the biological sense is manifest in the conscious life of man. If there be a relationship, we can never be sure that we are able to determine precisely what that relationship is. Simply by the very fact that a particular phenomenon is being observed, however accurately or inaccurately, the phenomenon itself undergoes change—even as does the observer.

As long as I can recall reacting to the experiences of life, I have observed in myself a tendency—even more, an inner demand—for "whole-making," a feel for a completion in and of things, for inclusive consummation. Experiences must somehow fit together; they must make sense to the mind. Many years ago when our two daughters were very small, the older one was explaining to the younger the meaning of Good Friday. She was given a very interesting and convincing account of the story of Jesus leading up to and including the crucifixion. But the younger child remained unsatisfied, and after more than thirty years I can hear still her impatient and frustrated cry: "But why did they have to kill him. . . . Why?" The events somehow had to fit together.

To try to make sense out of my concern for community and to honor intelligently its profound urgency in the human spirit are at last the feelings that sent me forth in the quest that these pages record. In my search I have examined, within the limitations of my skills, the insights inherent in the myths concerning the creation of the world—those query stories found among all peoples and all cultures as they sought to answer the old, old, yea timeless questions: "Why was I born? How did the world get started? Where did the animals and men come from? What was before when there were no men, when there were no animals? Was there anything at all before there was a world?"

I have looked long and hard at the early alienations of my youth; I have lived, as many others, through the frustration of alienation and rejection. I have had to discover, after the pattern of the grain in my wood, the difference between solitariness and loneliness. I have had to wrestle with many spiritual crises growing out of what seemed to be the contradictory demands of love and hate, of vengeance and mercy, and of retaliation and reconciliation. In all of these experiences there is a part of me that seeks ever for harmony, for community, for unity and creative synthesis in conflicting relations; and an equally articulate urgency within me for withdrawal, for separateness, for isolation, and for aggression. For long years I have felt that the former rested primarily in the demands of my religious commitment, while the latter belonged to that of my inward parts that had never yielded to the imperious demands of the religious spirit. But more and more the makings of such a thoroughgoing dualism seemed not only intolerable but also the constructing of an essentially false dichotomy.

Thus I am driven to seek, if happily I may find, a basis for this "whole-making" tendency in myself and in my relations with the unfolding of life itself in the world. In other words, my search has led me to seek answers to the insistent question: Is the pull toward community both within myself and the world of men indigenous to life, or is it a mirage, a delusion? To state the question a little differently: Is there some basis external to ones-self for the hopes and dreams of harmonious relations between men of whatever kind, state, or condition? Does the validity of the whole-making tendency in human life rest finally upon empirical sanction, or is it really against the drift, the movement of life as we experience it?

Thus I begin with the obvious proposition that I am not alien to life. I am a creature grounded and rooted in creatureliness. Therefore I am a participant in the life process rather than being an isolate within it. Truly, I am a space binder; as I described earlier, my body participates completely in the life process and it is nourished and sustained by ancient processes as old as life, and set in motion before any awareness of or knowledge about them was in evidence. As a creature, I am the inheritor of age-old wisdom. Hence there can be no sense of self on the part of the individual where there is no self-conscious experience of the body as one's own unique, private, and peculiar possession. The body is a man's intimate dwelling place; it is his domain as nothing else can ever be. It is coextensive with himself. If for any reason whatsoever a man is alienated in his own body either by shame, outrage, or brutality, his sense of community within himself is rendered difficult, if not impossible. It is small wonder that one of the oldest creeds of the Christian faith carries the phrase: I believe in the resurrection of the body. For many believers the affirmation that death does not ultimately separate a man from his body makes of death a little thing.

One is reminded of the story of the little boy who was afraid of the dark when he was put to bed. His mother told him that it was perfectly safe because God was with him in the dark. All he needed to do was to pray to God and He would comfort him. But the boy was still afraid. At length he said to his mother, "Mummy, will you please ask God to put some skin on and then I will be alright."

The sense of self is rooted in the experience of man's body as his own. It is for this reason that when men wish to break the will, the inner entity of others, they resort to direct and violent cruelty upon their bodies. The aim here is to force a man to abdicate his body and thereby to become an alien in his own house. This cuts him off from the sustaining source of his own physical being; he becomes disembodied and to that extent beingless.

There is a vast difference between an attitude, for whatever reason, that undertakes to separate man from his root in nature and one that seeks to honor one's belonging to nature as a part of the total life process. The body shares with all living things the urgency to actualize its potential as a body. Is it not reasonable to suggest that the tendency of the mind for whole-making or "seeing whole," for seeking harmony, for community is rooted in the experience of the body that in turn is grounded in all of life? I think so.

Of course we do not know when mind, as such, appeared. It is too static and mechanical, in my view, to assume that at some point in time, by some act, decree or fiat, mind, appeared in man. Of course, no one knows what the fact is. Generations of men have accommodated themselves to the notion that seemed to belong best to the necessities of their thought and life. It has been most helpful to me in my search to think of a time when mind as a separate and conscious entity did not formally exist in the body. To state it crudely: the mind was bodybound but mind as such was not. Many years ago I embodied the idea in these lines:

Through slimy oozes of primeval ocean beds,
Man's body, a living thing,
Climbed slowly up the years.
By fitful steps it made its way:
    Swimming, crawling, climbing,
    No stage was skipped.
At last, held taut twixt earth and sky,
It stood upright to shout defiance to the hills . . .
The body was mature,
All vital organs seemed as one
Without consent of mind.

The mind was there; mind it was not:
Taxed to the limit of its power
It kept the body safe, alive from every harm.
With life more friendly, mind released,
Thus man a living spirit, woke.

In light of this assumption, and thinking of the mind as an entity in itself, the tendency to "see whole" seems inherent. Thus the necessity that all experience make sense and the feel for harmony is *sui generis* or given. The clue is to be found in the nature of mind itself. All experience, then, becomes raw material for harmony, for order, and the individual stands ever in immediate candidacy for such fulfillment. If this is true, then it follows that when a person actualizes his own potential he becomes whole, harmonized, or fulfilled. It must be recalled, however, that the potential itself is dynamic and without measure. Thus, actualizing potential must mean always "as to" some particular goal, dream, or projection. In this sense a man's journey into life may be characterized as a quest for community within himself. As life realizes itself in human beings, what results is at the self-conscious level not unlike what happens instinctually in so-called subhuman forms of life.

At this point I amplify the point made in Chapter 1. It may not seem too far-fetched to examine a man's need to be loved, to be understood, to be cared for as the essential building blocks for the actualizing of his potential and the essential stuff of community among men. Every human being needs and is deeply nourished by the feeling of being cared for, of being dealt with totally or completely. There is an inexhaustible assurance of well-being that floods the life when one is aware of being touched at a center in one's self that is beyond all good and evil, beyond all merit and demerit. This is true without regard to culture, background, or condition. There is an insistent connection between the need for well-being and the elemental necessity in all forms of life to actualize its own potential and thus fulfill itself.

The phrase "tender loving care," commonly referred to as TLC, describes a certain kind of treatment that may characterize a relationship between one human being and another or between one human being and some other form of life. Such treatment results in an inner sense of harmony and stability that makes for growth and fulfillment. A wide range of laboratory experiments with rats and mice in recent years indicates quite dramatically that there is a radical difference between the behavior of those that are given TLC and those that are not. One such report suggests that the gentled rats were relatively immune to the effects of strain and deprivation because there was probably a decrease of ACTH output from the pituitary glands, with less release of hormones from the adrenal glands, while the others showed nervous adrenal glands with the negative effects from such treatment. It is not necessary to go into this aspect of the discussion in greater detail. Suffice it to say that what applies to rats, etc., applies to babies and to men.

The place to look for the emergence of community in human life is in the primary social unit, the family. It is here that the child first becomes aware of himself as a person. It has often been said that a child is not born human but becomes human only in a human situation or context. I take this to mean that in the intimacy of the family the profound process of the unfolding of potential is set in motion. The goal of fulfillment appears on the far horizon and persists as the pull of the long-timed emotion of the ideal. The child may fail both within and without, but against that failure something wars, always pushing, always making its claim felt. It is the claim of the building blocks, the built-in demand of the mind, the insistence of the organism, the upward push of the racial memory, the glow of the prophets' demand and the dream of the seer; it is what in religion is often called the will of God as touching the life of man.

What happens if in the life of the child there is in the family no pivotal point around which positive self-awareness emerges? The child is apt to become permanently crippled. This period of the child is also characterized as a time of innocence. In that sense there is the recapitulation of the story of the race as found in the various creation myths or query stories. For the child, very important things are happening in his organism, for the track is being laid the life journey of the body. In terms of community, this means that if the child is forced by the circumstances of his life to cope with his environment as if he were an adult, his very nervous system becomes enraged and an utter sense of alienation is apt to become the style of his life. Because he is rejected by life he begins to reject himself. The process of withdrawal and alienation begins its deadly operation before the child has any tools for assessing or interpreting what is happening to him. As an unconscious windbreak against this kind of communal suicide, provisions are made within the scope of the culture for giving children an early sense of belonging to the group as a whole and to a primary group within the larger relationships that give character to the total society.

There seems to be a built-in resistance in all human beings against the threat of isolation. It is a major safeguard against the disintegration of the self, for we cannot abide being cut off. And it is in the primary experience of family that the stage is set for the constant renewing and sustaining of the private life of the individual. Here the raw materials are provided for establishing an inner climate for the growth of personality and for giving full scope to the inner urge for whole-making that in turn increases the possibility for actualizing the potential of the individual. For in such a setting the individual not only has an awareness of being cared for, but also the way is opened for him to emerge as a person in an enlarged relationship of persons, the family.

In some societies, for what may be a wide range of reasons, the concept of the extended family has developed. This means that no member of the family, in substance, is ever lost. One evening in Nigeria, Mrs. Thurman and I were being entertained after a public address by an official of the Western Region. Our host offered us a soft drink, ginger beer. When he opened the bottle, but before serving us, he poured just a little on the floor, saying, "To my ancestors." For just one swirling moment I felt as if I were surrounded by a host of others who were suddenly a part of this moment of celebration. In modern life such a concept bristles with intense complications. However it is but another manifestion, in fine, of the need for belonging, for being cared for, which, in turn, is instinctive to life itself and therefore cannot be ultimately affected by death. A way has to be found for honoring this urgency of life and the human spirit. The frustration of this tendency to wholeness in man is the withering blight that is making so much of modern life a wasteland.

The recognition of the continuing sense of belonging is not only present in the so-called ancestor but is also to be found in the total etiquette surrounding the experience of death. In some parts of the world I have seen the graves of deceased members of the family in the front yards of the family house. This symbolizes their continuing presence that even death cannot sever. Many funeral rites are suggestive in the same way. There are clues to this insistence in the sustaining way that mourning for the dead honors their presence in the midst of the living.

To be remembered is the point that the family group is a part of a larger social unit in an ever-widening circle of belonging. The importance of place, of territory, of the earth takes on special meaning. Man is a child of nature; he is rooted and grounded in the earth. He belongs to it, and it belongs to him. I remember hearing an Indian Chief from northwestern Canada say: "I come from away up North near the Arctic Circle. I am a part of the snow, ice, and wind in winter. These flow into me and I flow into them." Man cannot long separate himself from nature without withering as a cut rose in a vase. One of the deceptive aspects of mind in man is to give him the illusion of being distinct from and over against but not a part of nature. It is but a single leap thus to regard nature as being so completely other than himself that he may exploit it, plunder it, and rape it with impunity.

This we see all around us in the modern world. Our atmosphere is polluted, our streams are poisoned, our hills are denuded, wild life is increasingly exterminated, while more and more man becomes an alien on the earth and a fouler of his own nest. The price that is being exacted for this is a deep sense of isolation, of being rootless and a vagabond. Often I have surmised that this condition is more responsible for what seems to be the phenomenal increase in mental and emotional disturbances in modern life than the pressures—economic, social, and political—that abound on every hand. The collective psyche shrieks with the agony that it feels as a part of the death cry of a pillaged nature.

Nevertheless, the importance of territory in the experience of community remains. Territory is one of the perennial guarantors supporting man's experience of community. Man has to *feel* at home if he is to be nurtured; home means place and the place means territory.

In modern life the symbol of homeland that has emerged in full significance is that of sovereignty. Thus the state becomes the rallying point for establishing the meaning and the significance of the life of persons within its boundaries. This is the larger unity that guarantees the smaller primary and secondary units within its boundaries. This symbol of belonging seems to meet a deep need in the life of modern man in a manner somewhat unique in modern history. As such, it unifies the individual and supersedes all other integrating symbols; this is particularly true in a society where there is no state religion to share the sovereignty of the state. It provides a common tie for its citizens and a technical ground for rejecting aliens. It formally defines an outsider and establishes rites and rituals for belonging. Even where there are birthrights unique to those who are born within its boundaries, provisions are made for "categories of belonging" established by custom and guaranteed by laws that govern. In modern life it is sovereignty that finally has the power of veto and certification over the individuals who make up the common life.

Thus the state takes on a transcendent role, thereby fulfilling one of the basic requirements of a religion. It seeks to answer three basic needs of the human spirit: for a supreme object of devotion and therefore worship, for a way of thinking about and believing in the object of devotion, and for a way of life in which the spirit of the object of devotion is expressed. The assumption is that the citizen who is loyal to sovereignty experiences community. He lives in a climate in which it is reasonable to assume that his potential can be actualized or that life can under the circumstance or condition be given a maximum opportunity to realize itself in him. Such a notion of sovereignty does something more. It gives the citizen an integrated basis for his behavior so that there is always at hand a socially accepted judgment that can determine for him when he is lost, when he has missed the way—that is, when he is out of community. It defines the meaning of civic character and determines the kind of civic responsibility that may develop it. It may withhold such responsibility and thereby determine who may develop civic character, the true symbol of membership. Again, such a notion inspires a basis for a definition of self-sacrifice, not only of possessions, but also of life itself. If the sacrifice of life is made in defense of sovereignty, a man is given a special place of honor and recognition. If in defense of the integrity of sovereignty he takes the life of another, his guilt is short-circuited by the paeans of praise accorded to the hero. A curious and specious distinction is made between murder at the behest of sovereignty and murder without such sanction. Finally, the notion inspires a sense of participating in a collective or communal destiny, thus reaffirming in crisis a sense of belonging to a transcendent entity in which the individual life is somehow transformed into something so much more than itself.

There are many symbols and rituals of sovereignty by which the sense of community is kept current, fluid, and viable. Symbols such as a national flag and a national anthem or hymn come to mind. There is the ritual that is a part of the voting ceremony or etiquette, the varied celebrations to commemorate the nation's founding, the spontaneous or structured emotions surrounding the crises due to war with other sovereignties, etc. But one of the most dramatic rituals for highlighting the sense of belonging is the device of national or universal registration, when, under conditions of limited supply of certain consumer goods, rationing becomes mandatory. It is most interesting to observe that when our own Sovereign State made such a demand of citizens, many of them felt themselves a a vital part of the common life for the first time in their lives. Up until then, many whose names included such initials as J. B., for instance, were now required by the state to give full names to such initials. To them it meant that the Sovereign State itself wanted to know precisely who they were as to both name and place. The demands of communal defense or communal aggression gave them a quickened sense of belonging and participation.

It can be very readily understood how the sovereignty of the state may create a major problem for the man of religion, the assumption being that such a man has a commitment and a sense of loyalty that may transcend his loyalty to the state, leading to an inescapable and fundamental conflict in loyalties. The very concept of sovereignty cannot accommodate itself to a divided loyalty in any sense that is absolute. Such a position is intolerable to both its integrity and stability. One of the practical though silent agreements between the state and religious institution is the recognition of separate spheres of influence over the life of the individual. Within the total territory for which sovereignty is responsible certain limited areas may be recognized as temporarily out of bounds for the state. In our country such a provision is made in the separation of church and state, as defined in the Constitution. The important thing here is to indicate that such a dualism is limited, and ultimately the power of veto and certification of the life of the individual rests with the state. An individual may abide by the judgment and take the consequences. There is a long history of those who reserved the right of veto and certification over their own lives, the authority of sovereignty to the contrary notwithstanding. But despite the varied avenues of appeal, of adjustment, of adjudication, the perogative of sovereignty is finally to say "yes" or "no," and to make it hold. The rationalization covering such an eventuality is that the sovereign *is* the people.

It becomes clear that if there are any citizens within the state who by definition, stated or implied, are denied freedom of access to the resources of community as established within the state, such persons are assailed at the very foundation of their sense of belonging.

It reaches in to affect what takes place even within the primary social unit, the family, where community is first experienced. The term "second class citizen" is often used to describe such a status. This means that such persons are "outsiders" living in the midst of "insiders," required to honor the same demands of sovereignty but denied the basic rewards of sovereignty. This collective or communal denial of the rights and the "rites" of belonging cuts deep into the fabric of the total life of the state. In the first place, it creates a condition of guilt in the general society that has to be absorbed in order to keep life tolerable within the body politic in general.

This becomes an increasingly critical issue as the relationships between sovereign states themselves become more competitive in the terrific crucible of power politics. It is here that the search for the jugular vein of one state is sought by another state of relatively equal strength and power on a steadily shrinking planet. The basic commodity in the play of power politics is for the extension of community of the particular states. The aim here is to bring those who are out of community into a vigorous sense of their own importance, thus inspiring the hope that in such acquiesence they will be able to realize their own potential. This is the essence of the critical struggle for the conquest of the minds and emotions of modern man. Given the loyalty and devotion of these, all other things follow: acceptance of standards of value, new wants for consumer goods immediately available, thereby making new markets—the list is endless. It is seen that the issue turns on the rewards for belonging. But if within the competing powers it can be clear, or is known, that within a given sovereignty there are those who are by birth insiders but are regarded or defined as outsiders notwithstanding, then those who stand in candidacy for belonging may be deterred, stymied, or sidetracked. In the light of this analysis, for instance, it is quite possible that in the major struggle between the Soviet Union and the United States of America the future belongs to that power which is the most convincing witness to the fact that it makes available to all its citizens the freedom of access to a social climate in which the individual not only has an authentic sense of belonging, but in which it is a reasonable hope for him to actualize his potential, thereby experiencing community within himself as part and parcel of the experience of community within the state.

The role of minorities in the modern state is crucial not only for the state as a community among world states, but also for the experience of community on the part of the minorities themselves. As suggested earlier, wherever citizens are denied the freedom of access to the resources that make for a sense of belonging, a sense of being totally dealt with, the environment closes in around them, resulting in the schizophrenic dilemma of being inside and outside at one and the same time. Or worse still, they are subject to the acute trauma of not knowing at any given moment whether they are outsiders or insiders. Such is the terrifying fate not only of the Afro-American but also of the Mexican-Latin American, the American Indian, and all those ethnic strains that make up the so-called Third World.

I shall permit myself two comments—one brief, the other extended—concerning the bearing of my thesis on community in the life of two of these minority groups.

I

The American Indian is the only indigenous people within the confines of American sovereignty. The merciless and ruthless attack on the ground of community in the life of the American Indian is completely amoral: To uproot him from territory that gave him a rare sense of belonging, in which he could actualize his potential within a frame of reference that was totally confirming, and at the same time to keep him in full or relative view of his devastated and desecrated extension of self that the land signified is a unique form of torture, a long, slow, anguished dying. The original insider is forced to become an outsider in his own territory. There are some things in life that are worse than death—surely this must be judged as such. The Indian wanders homeless and rootless as a fleeting ghost in and out of our dreams and like Banquo, is an invisible guest at both our times of feasting and our times of prayer. An unconscious guilt has entered namelessly into the very fiber of the American character and there is no catharsis to be found. Every time in our sovereign power we champion the cause of those who are uprooted in their own land and are forced to watch their souls wither and die without communal nourishment, there he stands in full view before our spirits while our words falter and our claim to challenge falls limp at our feet.

II

The search for community on the part of the Afro-American minority within the larger American community reveals still another facet of the inside-outside dilemma. Those interested in a more elaborate statement of my views should read my book *The Luminous Darkness,* an analysis of the anatomy of segregation and the ground of hope. Unlike the American Indian, the African slave was uprooted from his land, his territory, and brought forcibly several thousand miles away to another land completely alien to his spirit and his gods. All ties that gave him a sense of belonging, of counting, of being a person nourished by a community of persons were abruptly severed, lacerated, torn asunder. Bodies that were emotionally bleeding hulks were set down in the new world of the Americas. Initially he had no standing, even of that of outsider. In terms of his access to the sources of nourishment for community, initially he had none. No, not even the status of being a human being. It is no accident that the New Testament Greek word for slave is *soma,* which means body, a thing.

He was a part of the land, the territory. To that extent—and this is crucial—he was a part of the *ground* of community, the land by which the slave owner sought to realize his potential in community. Thus some measure of well-being to the slave could not be separated from the well-being of the slave owner. They were bound by the same chains. To some readers, such a distinction may seem merely academic and therefore unreal. For the slave, the primary social group, the family, rested always upon an unpredictable contingency. Most often the existence and the integrity of the family were ignored or destroyed when on the slave market all familial ties were like flotsam and jetsam on the tide of the angry waters of bartering. Those who lived on a given plantation were forced into a primary social group and gave what was available to the children in their midst, while their little wary egos squeezed their experiences for whatever could be found to nourish and sustain.

There were three currents flowing through the communal life of the plantation slave from which survival, sustenance, and nourishment could be drawn. The first was his tendency toward whole-feeling, to which much of our earlier discussion was devoted. It is one with the endless search for nourishment, inherent in even the simplest forms of life. Here there was no exception—the inner necessity to stake a claim for the self not only to nourish but also to sustain. Second, he needed some all-encompassing dimension to life, native to the spiritual needs of the human spirit and the raw materials brought into focus and synthesis by the religious mood. Third, he felt the drive, the tendency or urge expressed in aggression. Aggression cannot be separated from the urge for and to community. It may be that we get a grand and awesome preview of these two in the incipient ground of human behavior in what has been discovered about the behavior of the cell in seeking its own nourishment and rejecting, by an uncanny directed spontaneity, any intruder that is sensed as a threat to the inner cohesiveness of the structure of the cell. No understanding of the significance of community can escape the place and significance of aggression. Thus it was the operation of this trilogy in the life of the slave that made the forebears of the Afro-American of today endure the long night and greet the dawn with ancient awareness.

In the weary isthmus connecting the slave to the present there were many cataclysms: the War between the States, centering on the issue of slavery—a wide range of legal statutes defining and redefining the status and rights of the slaves and their descendents, which have continued down to latest times; at least two world wars, in which finally no distinction was made between combatants and noncombatants; the rise of communism and the appearance on the world scene of two world powers involving more than half of the earth's population, dedicated to one form or another of the dialectic of materialism, economic determinism, and the overthrowing of state religions; the rise and fall of two great fascist states committed to the armed conquest of the world; the ushering in of the atomic age by intiating the use of the atomic bomb in war and the creation of stockpiles of atomic weaponry sufficient to provide the equivalent of 30,000 tons of TNT explosives for every human being on the earth; the mechanization of life by phenomenal advances in technology; the real possibility of the discontinuity of life on the planet—the explorations of inner space; the immoral war in Vietnam—the list seems endless!

While all these things were happening, and not fundamentally unconnected with them, there was the general revolt of youth and their disenchantment with the society into which they were born. The result is that more and more they regard themselves as outsiders in the midst of the land of their roots and culture. In their acute alienation, they have a diminishing sense of belonging, do not feel themselves cared for and nurtured in a climate that makes the possibility of actualizing their potential remote, if at all possible. Two things characterize their mood and temper: one, they have no sense of place and are therefore rootless and disoriented in their contemporary environment, and two, the future has little if any meaning, for it is jeopardized by war and the threat of wars, with the fateful consequences of full-scale atomic racial suicide and the destruction of nature itself, without whose sustenance even the thought of survival comes to a grinding halt.

All these things have had a terrific impact on the life of the Afro-American in society. They have crucially affected his sense of belonging, which was always tenuous and fragile. Several considerations should be noted here. Together with the rest of America he is experiencing the collapse of the family structure—that primary womb out of which emerges the self-conscious urge to community —as a sense of belonging and support. It must be remembered that notwithstanding the family life's survival of the ravages of slavery, the struggle for individual economic survival in the turbulent waters of the period of reconstruction, the acute vulnerability of the family structure under the constant attack of lust, lasciviousness, and often secret affection of many of the white men of the South, and, from the turn of the century, the personality damage wrought by mounting segregation in the region and in the country as a whole, something very creative was at work deep within the social structure of Negro life. It was a counterdefense. The individual began to feel himself part of a larger primary structure in which kinship by blood was not a criterion for the claim of belonging. For a long time the Negro adult in the community stood *in loco parentis* to any Negro child. It was not necessary to know who the child was or where he lived. This gave the child an immediate sense of being cared for, with positive results in his own personality. The individual life could not be easily separated from the whole. Any stranger who came into the community had to be given hospitality, for all doors outside of the Negro community were closed to him. Thus there was the constant experience of overall identification. And this was good.

It broke down decisively and with devastating results, however, at one critical point—with the white community. The residue that accumulated in the collective and individual psyche of the black man from the awful sense, *that always, under any and all circumstances, his life was utterly at the mercy of the white world, is the most important, single clue to the phenomena of the present.* The most vicious, cruel, and amoral manifestation of this fact was lynching. The heartrending years when hundreds of Negroes were lynched, burned, and butchered by white men whose women and children were often special spectators of the inhuman ceremony are conveniently forgotten. It is scarcely remembered how long it took to pass antilynch legislation. The *bodies* of Negroes remember, and their psyches can never forget this vast desecration of personality. The boundaries of any sense of community, the effectiveness of one's life as a person, the breakdown of the instinctual tendency toward whole-making, the personality violence from aggression, thwarted and turned in on one's self, the searching felt in the presence of the humiliation of heroes, the guilt inspired by anonymous fears that live in the environment—these are some of the shadows, the unconscious reaction to which must be understood as we try to find community in the presence of the grim confrontations facing American society.

Concerning the society as a whole, much has been written and there will be much more as perspective is gained on the social events of the present time. As the older generation, we have suddenly become aware of our youth, as if for the first time. We are angered by their anger, even though secretly we marvel at the courage of their anger. We are frightened by their violence, even as we ponder it. We are shocked by their failure to respond to our values, even as we are humiliated by our own sense of failure and inadequacy. Nothing seems to hold. Nothing seems adequate to the crisis that is upon us. In our extremity we are tempted to take refuge in old shibboleths that we ourselves long since abandoned. We find ourselves using words that have been forsaken by meaning. At last it is beginning to dawn upon us, that at some time in the past—when, we are not sure—we became separated from our absolutes. It is from the life of our youth that we discover that we have lost our way. We, too, have little sense of belonging; our feel for whole-making has included less and less of the world, of the wide range of human life, until we are only sure of it as touching our family, particularly our children. Now, it often seems to us, they turn and rend us because we have sought to nourish them with the sense of our failure.

All of this applies to the older generation of Negroes, but with even greater intensity. In many ways they have tried to shield their children from naked exposure to the worst and most damaging aspects of white society. They have stood guard on the walls that separate and divide, seeking always how to make a virtue of social necessity. Often with sacrifices of which they dare not speak, they have bought time for their youth to prepare for effective living with tools, skills, and knowledge of which they sometimes dreamed but could never realize. Many of them uprooted themselves from a life that they knew, under circumstances with which they had learned to cope, in order that their children might have a wider range of opportunity and a cleaner chance to actualize *their* potential. Now they are faced with the bitter judgment of their own youth, denouncing them as cowards and fools because they were duped and betrayed by the very society from which they sought to protect them. This they sought to accomplish either by reducing the exposure of their youth to that society or by equipping them with a facility that might be exchanged in that society for certain prizes or immunities not available to the rest of their kind.

Meanwhile, these older ones were seeking ways and means for pushing back the boundaries by removing the walls that shut them in. What a long and often unrewarding struggle! The cry in the heart was for more room, more opportunity, more of a sense of belonging. Thus the circling series of confrontations, within and without any zones of agreement—the ballot, better schools, equal schools, the same schools, the freedom of access to the total life of the community on the same basis as other citizens—the list is long and wearisome, but whatever may have been the contradictions, they were never regarded as final. Many tried to keep before their view heroes and heroines of the past to bolster a sagging self-estimate in the present. But there was ever the insinuating circumstance, the heroes failed where they themselves had failed—they were outsiders—the walls, sometimes bold and direct, often soft-spoken and indirect, were ever present.

The heroic *quality* of life was not missing. But the precious ingredient had never been found to protect or immunize the hero from the final assault that would send him crashing to the ground! The hero had to be a man of courage, possessing the acumen of mind and the discipline of training that could stand up under the scrutiny of the sharpest critics who guarded the citadels of power upon which society based its security, prowess, and control. In addition he must be one whose sense of community was deep in the throb of Negro life so that between his heart and theirs there would be a swinging door that no man could shut. His thinking, his feelings, and his deeds must transcend all that separates and divides. He must know hate and conquer it with love; he must know fear and conquer it with strange new courage.

As a result of a series of fortuitous circumstances there appeared on the horizon of the common life a young man who for a swift, staggering, and startling moment met the demands of the hero. He was young. He was well-educated with the full credentials of academic excellence in accordance with ideals found in white society. He was a son of the South. He was steeped in and nurtured by familiar religious tradition. He had charisma, that intangible quality of personality that gathers up in its magic the power to lift people out of themselves without diminishing them. In him the "outsider" and the "insider" came together in a triumphant synthesis. Here at last was a man who affirmed the oneness of black and white under a transcendent unity, for whom community meant the profoundest sharing in the common life. For him, the wall was a temporary separation between brothers. And his name was Martin Luther King, Jr.

His star shot across the heavens like Haley's comet, making a mighty radiance in the light of which ancient dwellers in darkness could find their way to brotherhood. A fresh, cool wind blew across the desert places and the tired, the weary, the fearridden, the hated, and the haters could find a bold new courage. At last there was available a personal and collective catharsis. Here was a new hero who gave the assurance of succeeding at the very point that had proved so vulnerable to all the heroes of the past. As a special kind of grace, he had achieved this by the time the assassin's bullets struck him down. Never again would the boundaries be as established as they were before his coming. In his own short and intense life, the announcement was made to all and sundry, far and near, that the life of the black man was not at the mercy of white people. That for better or for worse they were tied together. No black man could be what his potential demanded unless the white man could be what *his* potential demanded. No white man could be what his potential demanded un¹ess the black man could be what *his* potential demanded. For him this was literal truth and therefore literal fact. The elements of a new residue began building up in the psyche of the black man. And this was good.

It is not my purpose here to discuss the deep polarizations within the black community that began to emerge; however, there are two important aspects in the subsequent unfolding of the whole-making tendency operative in Negro life. First, there was the emergence of other heroes. The psychological condition for testing the hero had been set forth in the dynamics of the social experience of the race. One of the characteristics of the awakening that followed the emergence of Martin Luther King was a search for other heroes whose magic would make room for the vital and fundamental place of aggresion, that deep drive in life so central to the life of the species. It is not merely protective, shielding to life, but it also has a prowling quality that can scarcely be distinguished from belligerence. In the light of this need, the drive could not be ignored—it had to be utilized, if not on behalf of community, then it was mandatory that a different concept of community must be created. Just as nonviolence had become the watchword of community in the first instance, violence became the watchword of the new concept.

What emerged as the new concept of community? The tendency toward whole-making was at once self-defeating if it did not establish clear-cut and fixed boundaries. Without such boundaries freedom itself had no significance, so the reasoning ran. Therefore, it was only within fixed boundaries, *self-determined*—and that is the key word—that the goals of community could be experienced, achieved, or realized. The natural lines along which the boundaries should be set would be to separate those who had been historically victimized by society from those who had victimized them. The bankruptcy of trust stood fully revealed. What had been whispered for so long behind closed doors about the real relation between black and white was now shouted in the streets and in the public forums, followed by the demand for radical separation between black and white. There was the strident insistence that any notion of inclusiveness was merest illusion, and the term "brainwashed" was applied to anyone with a contrary point of view. Such a separation was distinguished from segregation because it was voluntary and deliberate. Psychologically, it would utilize aggression in a manner positive and creative rather than positive and destructive. The way was clear now for the emergence of a new kind of hero, one who would be a new symbol—a profoundly angry man, hard and unyielding. Black now took on a new meaning and the term "Black Power" became a fresh rallying point for a sagging self-estimate. Nothing must be as it was before in school, church, marketplace, and territory. The winds blew sharp and fierce across the regions of American life.

This kind of self-estimate sent the believers back into the past, as far as human records extended. Africa became symbolic of the ideal, an ancient, yet historical expression of the new center for the integration of the human spirit. Many rituals appeared in varied forms—new styles of dress, of hair grooming and new forms of old culinary delights. Fresh words also entered the vocabulary—soul food, dashikis, and the Afro Hair dress, etc. In fine, the new sense of community made for the rejection *of* the white community rather than being rejected *by* the white community. A cause was made out of the latter rejection and a new offensive was born. The heroes were men and women who became at once the voices of that rejection. They were local, national, and international. The dream of a new sovereignty within the larger sovereignty became apparent. A new political structure within the larger political super-structure put in its challenging appearance.

There were other forms that the mood of the new sense of community found acceptable. The use of language became a complete mythology. Niceties and refinement of speech became anathema, for they were symbols of the world that was being rejected. "Vulgarity" became the trade mark of many who had freed themselves of the contamination of the white society. Often those who stood for the old sense of community and continued to work on its behalf were regarded as "Uncle Toms." The man who was concerned about such things as good will and love beyond the new community was seen increasingly as a "traitor" to the new order. "Black is beautiful" became not merely a phrase—it was a stance, a total attitude, a metaphysic. In very positive and exciting terms it began undermining the idea that had developed over so many years into a central aspect of white mythology: that black is ugly, black is evil, black is demonic; therefore black people are ugly, evil, and demonic. In so doing it fundamentally attacked the front line of defence of the myth of white supremacy and superiority. The point at which to start would be with the children. Thus there would be a penetration into the seedbed where ideas are planted, nurtured, and developed. There began to appear new centers for black children that were not much concerned about the traditional tools of learning—reading, writing and arithmetic—as they were about uprooting and replanting. That is fundamental.

In order to document this new mood for a radically different sense of community, a rereading of history became urgent. Such a concern was not new in itself nor was it particularly novel. There were many voices from the past that had insisted upon correcting the distortions of the story of the black man in the western world and in the Americas. But the voices did not carry far because they were confined largely to the sophisticated, the most literate, and, above all, to the specialists. Now all of this had to be changed; the fresh word about the past had to take to the streets, giving rise to an informed public mind both within and beyond the black community. It had to be a common knowledge that would generate mass enthusiasm for building a different collective self-image, thus providing stature for the design to stake out territory in the domain previously dominated and controlled by white society. Such a reexamination of the roots of history did not exclude the origins of the common religion, Christianity. This emphasis found its most arresting statement in the Black Manifesto delivered to the churches, and in the concepts of the Black Jesus and the Black Madonna.

Overall, there has been the reaction of stubborn resistance, shudders of guilt, wary capitulation, and desperate efforts to understand and comprehend. The behavior of the cells of the body in the presence of the radical invasion of other cells from foreign bodies as seen in organ transplants *may be* mute testimony to the ground of such behavior in personality.

The summary above must suffice to indicate the profound seriousness of the new concept of community as it emerged in Negro life. The recognition of the instinctual tendency to whole-making and the utilization of the equally basic drive manifested in aggression were both being expressed in establishing and defending the boundaries separating black from white. It cannot be overemphasized that the emergence of the new African states in the arena of world states and their place of influence in the United Nations must not be separated from the new concept of community appearing in the black community.

Let my meaning be clear. What we see happening is the deliberate, carefully delineated effort to create within white society a community of separateness within which an attempt is being made to establish a dependable sense of black autonomy, to make articulate a collective sense of self, capable of nourishing and supporting the individual as he works out his destiny in American society and the world. In order to do this, it has seemed necessary to reduce exposure to all white persons to a minimum and to recognize, in fact, that the white man is the *enemy*, as is indicated by his historic treatment of the black man. The assumption is that such a pragmatic possibility is quite realistic. It can be carried out with or without his cooperation, peacefully if possible, violently if necessary. Inasmuch as he has used fear most effectively in the past, in his effort to establish and maintain throughout his society artificial and arbitrary boundaries between himself and nonwhites, others may use the same instrument to establish and maintain self-determined boundaries between black and white. The white community has held the black community in place by the threat of violence, backed always by the power to implement it and to carry it out.

This means that he is psychologically and precisely vulnerable to the same tactical maneuver. Violence is his most acceptable instrument for both control and social change as he may determine it. The difference in access to and the availability of the tools of violence between the black and white communities *must* not be permitted to blunt the appeal or deflate the enthusiasm. So the argument runs.

One more step in this rather long summarizing critique must be taken. What has been the overall effect of this concept of community on American society in general? I suppose the social historian or psychologist would have an impressive and exhaustive list. I would make this observation. There have been far-reaching effects in accommodating the impact on white society. Many doors that have been closed and sealed are now open. This is true not merely because of the impact of the new pressure, but also because the pressure itself has provided opportunity for doing what apparently could not have been done before without good, sufficient, and defensive reasons. Vast areas of society that have been aware of but not affected by Negro life have let such awareness become effective in many changes within the social patterns and structures.

In many ways the antiblack hatemongers have become legitimatized and, in many instances but by no means in all, violence and brutality against Negroes have been given moral and social sanction. By vocal and, most often, silent consent the cry for Law and Order is given a specific, racially sinister meaning. The sanctity of sovereignty, as discussed earlier, expressed in the power of the state to exercise veto and certification over the lives of its citizens, is declared to be in jeopardy, and Order is separated from and given precedence over Justice. The will to segregate that is inherent in the structure of American society is more and more stripped of its disguises and making itself felt without its customary façades; at the same time all kinds of people in the larger society are being aroused to make their voices heard and their power felt on behalf of the creation of an American society inclusive of all. Such persons make the rejection of the more narrowly fixed and self-determined boundaries of the black community their strength and incentive. Up to and including the present time, no creative way has been found to accomplish the specific ends of identity and healthy self-estimate that is devoid of the negativisms that seem to be inherent in the present struggle.

There are those who interpret what is happening as the work of a few radicals and hotheads. They cannot see in the stirrings anything that is symptomatic of the shifting of the ground of society that makes for cataclysm and upheaval. The notion suggests that if the leaders can be eliminated, jailed, or even killed, it would restore what is regarded as a lost harmony among the races. Others declare that a sickness has overtaken the society as a whole, and what we are observing is but symptomatic of something far more disturbing in the common life. There are still others—they are always to be found—who seek to exploit the unrest and the zeal for the sense of limited community on behalf of ideologies that are foreign to the soil of America; a new kind of outsider from another social climate is busily at work carrying out his evil design. This sense of jitters allows hidden anxieties to surface themselves with many hideous, ugly, and threatening faces. It is the time and the moment when the alarmist comes into his own, but the cry is far removed from the real source of the ferment.

It is not amiss to be reminded that there may be many areas of life within the black community that are disturbed at the turn of events. Perhaps the sharpest criticism is the seeming ignorance of the champions for self-determined separateness concerning the struggles of the past. The paradox is as cruel as it is apparent. On the one hand there is the insistence of reinterpretation of, and at the same time, a rejection of past history. This evident lack of a sense of history is a most damaging criticism. There seems to be no recognition of the relentless logic tying present events and ideas with what has preceded them and from which they can never be separated. The cavalier manner in which this seems to be ignored is seen as being the merest stupidity and ignorance. There is general alarm over the way in which the aggression turns on itself, inflicting havoc and wreckage on Negroes themselves. There are many who have lived deep in the heart of American society and know with certainty that to undertake to build community as a closed entity within the large society is not only suicidal but the sheerest stupidity, because it plays directly into the hands of those persons and elements in society who have stood as defenders against any and all inclusiveness as the true (American) basis of community. What they were unable to accomplish after three hundred years is now being done for them without their having to lift a finger. They are willing to encourage, to support with their money and their power all moves toward separating black from white. At last, their message has gotten through to Negroes and is being implemented by them in a manner not to be envisioned by the wildest flight of the imagination.

One of the most disturbing features of this total activity is its effect on youth. There is widespread feeling and thought that the youth are being used by clever men, many of whom are motivated by unselfish concerns and dedication, to sacrifice the youth while their minds are undeveloped and they have no survival skills that enable them to cope with their environment in the future. The notion that such youth are expendable is as cruel as it is self-defeating.

But there is one indictment against the older generation that the present movement brings into focus: Black youth have not been given a binding sense of identity—this is not confined to them exclusively—and there have been few avenues open to them for having a sense of membership in society as a whole. But the new and limited sense of community, whose boundaries are self-imposed, has provided two things: (1) *a basis for identity with a cause and a purpose more significant to them than their own individual survival, and* (2) *a feeling of membership with others of common values with whom they can experience direct and intense communication.* When they hear that call they drop their tools and answer! No amount of logic, argumentation, intimidation, or appeal has meaning where those precious ingredients are lacking. I feel that here is the clue to the appeal that the new community makes to youth. Among the youth are not merely to be found those who are not standing in immediate candidacy for higher learning, whose direct prospects for the actualizing of their potential is without promise of fulfillment. There are others who have the skills already, whose minds are disciplined for finding some measure of fulfillment in society as it is now constituted. Two of the most important tests of community are met here—a basis for integrated action or behavior with which the individual may, can, and, finally, must identify and a sense of membership in and belonging to a company of others who are held together by common values, ideals, and commitments. White society has not only shut them out of such involvement (except at times when the stern Voice of Sovereignty sends forth the call to arms in defense of ideas or ideals to which they do not have the freedom of access and therefore with which identification is not easy), but also it has robbed them of any sense of belonging in the present or in any imaginable future. Therefore, the new sense of community within self-determined boundaries seems the most realistic and immediately practical solution to a cruel and otherwise seemingly insoluble problem.

It is my considered judgment that the present solution is a stopgap, a halt in the line of march toward full community or, at most, a time of bivouac on a promontory overlooking the entire landscape of American society. It is time for assessing and reassessing resources in the light of the most ancient memory of the race concerning community, to hear again the clear voice of prophet and seer calling for harmony among all the children of men. At length there will begin to be talk of plans for the new city—that has never before existed on land or sea. At the center of the common life there will be strange and vaguely familiar stirrings. Some there will be whose dreams will be haunted by forgotten events in which in a moment of insight they saw a vision of a way of life transcending all barriers alien to community. Among the elder statesmen will be those through whose blood the liquid fires of Martin Luther King's dream swept all before it in one grand surge of beatific glory. They will remember and wonder at what they see about them. It will be discovered, how long and under what circumstance will remain among the mysteries, that the barriers of community can never be arbitrarily established, however necessitous it may be to seek to do so for good and saving reasons. Here and there will be those who will walk out under the stars and think lonely thoughts about whence they came and the meaning that their presence in the heavens inspires. They will wonder and ponder heavy thoughts about man and his destiny under the stars. One day there will stand up in their midst one who will tell of a new sickness among the children who in their delirium cry for their brothers whom they have never known and from whom they have been cut off behind the self-imposed barriers of their fathers. An alarm will spread throughout the community that it is being felt and slowly realized that community cannot feed for long on itself; it can only flourish where always the boundaries are giving way to the coming of others from beyond them—unknown and undiscovered brothers. Then the wisest among them will say: What we have sought we have found, our own sense of identity. We have an established center out of which at last we can function and relate to other men. We have committed to heart and to nervous system a feeling of belonging and our spirits are no longer isolated and afraid. We have lost our fear of our brothers and are no longer ashamed of ourselves, of who and what we are—Let us now go forth to save the land of our birth from the plague that first drove us into the "will to quarantine" and to separate ourselves behind self-imposed walls. For this is why we were born: Men, all men belong to each other, and he who shuts himself away diminishes himself, and he who shuts another away from him destroys himself. And all the people said *Amen.*

Bibliography

From among the extensive literature covering this field of inquiry, I have selected a few books which were most helpful in my investigation. They may prove of interest to the reader who wishes to explore the subject further.

Ardrey, Robert. *African Genesis.* New York: Atheneum, 1961, page 84.

Beadle, George and Muriel. *The Language of Life.* New York: Doubleday Anchor, 1967.

Berneri, Marie Louise. *Journey through Utopia.* Boston: Beacon Press, 1950.

Bible (King James Version). Genesis 1—4; Isaiah 11:1–9; (Moffatt translation) Revelation 20:11–13, 21:2–4 and 10 ff.

Boone, J. Allen. *Kinship with All Life.* New York: Harper & Row, 1954.

———. *The Language of Silence.* New York: Harper & Row, 1970.

Byrd, Richard E. *Alone.* New York: G. P. Putnam's Sons, 1938, pages 26, 183.

Cleague, Albert. *Black Messiah.* New York: Sheed & Ward, 1968.

Cone, James H. *Black Theology and Black Power.* New York: Seabury Press, 1969.

Cruse, Harold. *The Crisis of the Negro Intellectual.* New York: William Morrow & Company, 1967.

Di Pirajno, Alberto Denti. *A Grave for a Dolphin.* London: Andre Deutsch, 1956, pages 85 ff. ("A Sermon for Wart Hogs").

Dubkin, Leonard. *The White Lady.* New York: G. P. Putnam's Sons, 1952, pages 144–45.

Eiseley, Loren C. "The Secret of Life." *Harper's Magazine,* October, 1953.

————. *The Unexpected Universe.* New York: Harcourt, Brace & World, 1969.

Frank, Lawrence K. *Nature and Human Nature.* New Brunswick: Rutgers University Press, 1951, pages 42–43.

Gregory, Susan. *Hey, White Girl!* New York: Lancer Books, 1970.

Grobstein, Clifford. *The Strategy of Life.* San Francisco: W. H. Freeman, 1964, pages 25, 27.

Herbert, Don, and Bardossi, Fulvio. *Secret in the White Cell.* Case History of a Biological Search. New York: Harper & Row, 1969.

Hotchner, A. E. *Papa Hemingway.* A Personal Memoir. New York: Random House, 1955, pages 29–30.

Jeffers, Robinson. "The Inhumanist." From *The Double Axe and Other Poems,* Part 2. New York: Random House, 1948, pages 52–54.

Keen, William W. *I Believe in God and in Evolution.* Philadelphia: J. B. Lippincott Company, 1922, pages 29 ff.

Leach, Maria. *The Beginning.* Creation Myths Around the World. New York: Funk and Wagnalls, 1956.

Lester, Julius. *Search for the New Land.* New York: Dial Press, 1969.

Miller, Hugh. *The Community of Man.* New York: The Macmillan Company, 1949.

Montagu, M. F. Ashley. *The Direction of Human Development.* New York: Harper & Row, 1955.

Moore, Francis D. *Give and Take.* The Development of Tissue

Transplantation. New York: Doubleday & Company, 1964, pages 19 ff.

Morris, Desmond. *The Human Zoo.* New York: McGraw-Hill Book Company, 1969.

Mumford, Lewis. *The Story of Utopias.* Gloucester (Mass.): Peter Smith, 1959, pages 15, 78.

Negley, Glenn, and Patrick, J. Max. *The Quest for Utopia.* An Anthology of Imaginary Societies. Garden City: Anchor Books, 1962.

Nixon, Justin, and Hudson, Winthrop. *Christian Leadership in a World Society.* Rochester (N.Y.): Colgate-Rochester Divinity School, 1945.

Northrop, F. S. C. *Man, Nature and God,* New York: Simon & Schuster, 1962.

Plato. *The Republic of Plato.* Translated with introduction and notes by Francis MacDonald Cornford. New York: Oxford University Press, 1957.

Rush, Joseph Harold. *The Dawn of Life.* New York: Signet Science Library, 1962, pages 42–43.

Sanderson, Ivan T. *The Dynasty of Abu.* A History and Natural History of the Elephants and Their Relatives. New York: Alfred A. Knopf, 1962.

Schreiner, Olive. *Dreams.* Boston: Little, Brown, n.d., page 84.

Schuchter, Arnold. *Reparations.* The Black Manifesto and Its Challenge to White America. Philadelphia: J. B. Lippincott Company, 1970.

Sherrington, Charles. *Man On His Nature.* 2d ed. London: Cambridge University Press, 1953, pages 94–95.

Sinnott, Edmund W. *The Biology of the Spirit.* London: Victor Gollancz, 1956.

———. *The Bridge of Life.* New York: Simon & Schuster, 1966.

———. *Cell and Psyche.* The Biology of Purposes. New York: Harper & Row, 1961.

Smith, Russell Gordon. *Fugitive Papers.* New York: Columbia University Press, 1930, pages 4–5.

Steger, Jane. *Leaves from a Secret Journal.* Boston: Little, Brown & Company, 1926, pages 38-39, 83-84.

Thurman, Howard. *The Luminous Darkness.* A Personal Interpretation of the Anatomy of Segregation and the Ground of Hope. New York: Harper & Row, 1965.

Waters, Frank. *Book of the Hopi.* New York: Viking Press, 1963, pages 3-23.